ALBANIA
in Pictures

Thomas Streissguth

Twenty-First Century Books

Contents

Website address: www.lernerbooks.com

Twenty-First Century Books
A division of Lerner Publishing Group, Inc.
241 First Avenue North
Minneapolis, MN 55401 U.S.A.

web enhanced @ www.vgsbooks.com

CULTURAL LIFE   46

► Art. Architecture. Music. Language. Literature.
Religion. Food. Sports. Holidays and Festivals.

THE ECONOMY   58

► Services. Agriculture. Industry. Foreign Trade.
Transportation. Communications. The Future.

FOR MORE INFORMATION

Library of Congress Cataloging-in-Publication Data

Streissguth, Thomas, 1958–
      Albania in pictures / by Tom Streissguth.
      p. cm. — (Visual geography series. Second series)
      Includes bibliographical references and index.
      ISBN 978-0-7613-4629-6 (lib. bdg. : alk. paper)
      1. Albania—Juvenile literature. 2. Albania—Geography—Juvenile literature. 3. Albania—Pictorial works—
Juvenile literature. I. Title.
   DR910.S77 2011
   949.65—dc22   2009049953

Manufactured in the United States of America
1 – BP – 7/15/10

INTRODUCTION

Albania is a small nation in southeastern Europe. Within its borders lie sandy beaches, fertile lowlands, dense forests, and rugged mountains. Wolves, bears, and lynx inhabit the nation's woods. Eagles soar over its mountains. Many kinds of fish and waterfowl live in its waters.

Albania has a long, turbulent history. Many powerful empires and ambitious rulers have sought to control its strategic location at the crossroads of Europe and Asia. Albania lies beside a strait (narrow channel of water) linking the Adriatic and Ionian seas, which together form an arm of the Mediterranean Sea.

Modern Albanians claim descent from the Illyrians. About three thousand years ago, Illyrian society took shape on the Balkan Peninsula. This peninsula (finger of land) lies roughly between modern Italy and Turkey. In the 600s B.C., the ancient Greeks began building towns along Illyria's coast. Five centuries later, Illyria became the province of Illyricum within the powerful Roman Empire, based on the Italian Peninsula.

During the Roman era, outsiders began calling Illyrians the Albani, the name of one Illyrian tribe. In addition, the Christian religion arrived in Albania.

The collapse of the western half of the Roman Empire in the A.D. 400s left the Balkan region in turmoil. For the next thousand years, the Albanians lived in a feudal society. Landowners claimed the harvest and the military service of people living on their estates.

In the 1400s, Ottoman Turks invaded the Balkan Peninsula from Asia Minor (modern Turkey). They introduced Islam, a religion founded in Arabia in the 600s by the prophet Muhammad. Under Ottoman rule, about two-thirds of Albanians converted to Islam. The rest remained Christians. This religious split continued into modern times.

In 1912 Albania declared independence from the Ottoman Empire. But Albanian leaders held little authority in the region. A group of leaders from stronger European nations drew Albania's borders to suit their own needs. This act stranded millions of Albanians in neighboring countries.

Albania

- —— International border
- ⊛ Capital city
- • City
- ∴ Archaeological site

0   25 Miles
0   25 KM

N

SERBIA

MONTENEGRO

KOSOVO

White Drin River

Viçidol

Lake Fierzë

Lake Shkodër

Shkodër

Drin River

Lake Vaut të Dejës

Black Drin River

Shëngjin

Lezhë

Lake Ulzës

Bojana River

Mat River

MACEDONIA

Adriatic Sea

Durrës

Tiranë

Elbasan

Shushicë

Lake Ohrid

Shkumbin River

Lushnjë

Cërujë

Lake Prespa

Apollonia

Berat

Osum River

Voskopojë

Little Lake Prespa

Korçë

Vjosë River

Bay of Vlorë

Vlorë

ITALY

Strait of Otranto

Vjosë River

Drino River

Gjirokastër

Sarandë

Butrint

GREECE

Ionian Sea

0   500 Miles
0   500 KM

ATLANTIC OCEAN

EUROPE

ALBANIA

AFRICA

During World War I (1914–1918) and World War II (1939–1945), Albania became a battleground. Larger nations sought to control Albania's strategic port cities.

After World War II ended, Albanians took control of Albania. Their leader was Enver Hoxha. Hoxha feared another foreign invasion. He was also determined to build a pure Communist state. (Communism is a political and economic system whose goal is to distribute wealth fairly among people.) He outlawed non-Communist political organizations. He ruthlessly stamped out opposition. To build self-reliance and prevent foreign influence, Hoxha gradually cut ties with other nations.

Albania has one of the cleanest coastlines in the Mediterranean region. The Communist government feared invasion, so it created military zones along the coast. It forbade tourism and development of new towns or resorts. Outside the cities, the coast remains much as it was thousands of years ago.

By the early 1980s, Albania had no foreign trade or political allies. Hoxha's policies had stopped all foreign investment. Manufacturing declined. Shortages of food and factory goods grew common. In 1985, when Hoxha died, Albania was the poorest nation in Europe.

In the early 1990s, Albania's Communist regime fell. In 1992 a democratic government promised to reform the nation's economy. (A democratic government is made up of freely elected representatives.) But Albanians still struggled to find work and to survive. In 1997 many families lost their life savings in an illegal investment scheme the government had approved. Widespread rioting ensued. About two thousand people died. Albania's government nearly collapsed.

By 2000 Albania's economy began growing. The country's isolation had come to an end. Modern Albania trades actively with Greece, Italy, and other neighbors. In 2009 Albania joined the North Atlantic Treaty Organization (NATO), a defensive military alliance. That year Albania also applied for membership in the European Union (EU), an economic and political alliance of nearly thirty nations.

Albania remains one of Europe's poorest nations. It has little industry. Many of its 3.2 million people cannot find jobs. The nation faces a long journey toward political stability and prosperity. Nevertheless, Albania has attracted some investment in its energy resources and infrastructure (public works, such as roads). It is also developing tourism along its coast.

THE LAND

The Republic of Albania lies on the Balkan Peninsula in southeastern Europe. To the northwest is Montenegro. In the northeast lies Kosovo. Albania's eastern neighbor is Macedonia. Greece lies to the south.

A long arm of the Mediterranean Sea forms a 225-mile (362-kilometer) coastline in western Albania. The Strait of Otranto, which is about 47 miles (75 km) across at its narrowest point, separates Albania from the heel of boot-shaped Italy. North of the strait is the Adriatic Sea. South of the strait is the Ionian Sea.

Albania covers 11,100 square miles (28,748 sq. km), about the same size as the U.S. state of Hawaii. Albania stretches about 211 miles (340 km) at its longest point from north to south. Its widest point from east to west spans about 93 miles (150 km).

▶ Topography

Two main regions make up Albania's topography, or landscape. These are the Coastal Lowlands in the west and the Eastern Highlands.

Albania's Coastal Lowlands lie along the Mediterranean coast. This plain, or flatland, stretches about 120 miles (193 km) along western Albania from Lake Shkodër in the northwest to the city of Vlorë in the south. It reaches about 30 miles (48 km) inland, roughly to the city of Elbasan.

The lowlands are flat and sandy. Beaches and lagoons line the coast. A lagoon—an area of relatively shallow, quiet seawater—has access to the sea. But a lagoon is separated from the sea by some landform, such as a sandbar. Rivers flowing toward the coast from the mountains carry silt (fine soil) downstream. As they approach the ocean, the rivers split into several branches and form muddy deltas. The Myzeqe Plain on the central coast is a broad area of swamps and farmland.

The mountains of Albania's Eastern Highlands region separate Albania from all its neighbors. Many rivers and streams flow west through the gorges and valleys among these mountains. The highlands are composed of four mountain ranges. These are the North Albanian Alps, the Cukali Highlands, the Central Highlands, and the Southern Highlands.

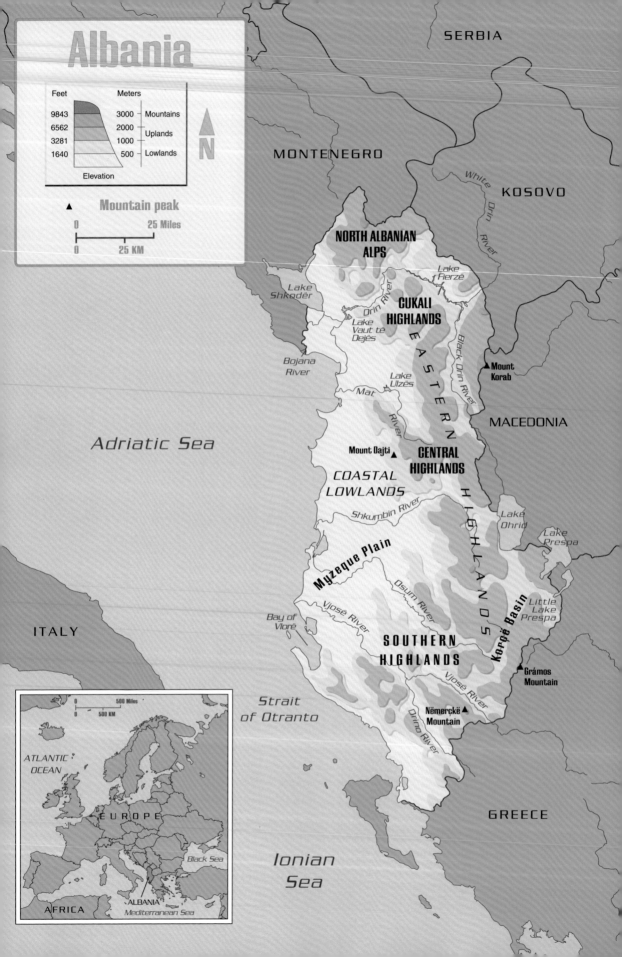

Albania's highest point, **Mount Korab,** lies on the border of Albania and Macedonia. The peak rises near the largest artificial lake in Albania, Lake Fierzë.

The North Albanian Alps extend 20 miles (32 km) southward from Montenegro. Ancient glaciers (slow-moving ice masses) carved the deep valleys of this range. Snow covers the highest ridges throughout the year. Isolated settlements dot these rugged mountains. Scattered pastures provide some grazing land for livestock. Most of the region is too steep and rocky for growing crops.

South of these mountains lie the grassy slopes and rounded peaks of the Cukali Highlands. These hills overlook the valley of the Black Drin River.

The Central Highlands stretch about 70 miles (113 km) from the Drin River to the Shkumbin River. Elevations there average about 2,000 feet (610 meters) above sea level. Some peaks reach 5,000 feet (1,524 m). Mount Korab, Albania's highest point, rises 9,068 feet (2,764 m) on the Macedonian border. A few narrow, twisting roads link the Central Highlands to the Coastal Lowlands. Most of the people in this area live in the river valleys and in small mountain basins (plains surrounded by higher elevations).

The Southern Highlands extend from the Shkumbin River into northern Greece. Within the eastern part of the range lies the Korçë Basin. Vineyards and fruit orchards crowd this plain. It is an important Albanian farming region. Southwest of the plain, the Nëmerçkë and the Grámos mountains tower over the Vjosë River valley. This valley serves as an important travel route between Albania and Greece. The Southern Highlands stretch all the way to the coast, south of the city of Vlorë.

▷ Rivers and Lakes

Albania has many rivers. They wind westward among the highlands and across the lowlands, eventually emptying into the sea. They carry a great deal of sediment (bits of solid material, like dirt) down from the highlands. Much of it lands in lowland marshes lining the rivers.

The marshy wetlands are unsuitable for farming. So in the early 1900s, Albania began a land reclamation program. Workers drained hundreds of coastal swamps to create farmland. Modern lowland farmers use the rivers to irrigate (water) their crops. Canals (artificial waterways) carry water from the rivers to the farm fields. Albania also uses some of its river power to generate electricity.

The Drin is Albania's longest river. It has two main tributaries (feeder streams). These are the White Drin, which rises in Kosovo, and the Black Drin, which begins in Macedonia. From the source of the White Drin to the sea, the river is 208 miles (335 km) long. It crashes through several narrow gorges in the highlands. Three hydroelectric dams along the highland course of the Drin create two large reservoirs (artificial lakes): Lake Fierzë and Lake Vaut të Dejës.

After it enters the lowlands, the Drin branches into two main channels. One channel empties into the Adriatic Sea near the town of Lezhë. The other channel joins the Bojana River.

The Bojana River links Lake Shkodër, which straddles the Montenegro border, to the Adriatic Sea. It is the only river in Albania deep enough for commercial boat traffic.

The Drin River winds through farm fields as it makes its way across northern Albania.

Vacationers crowd this beach on Lake Ohrid, one of Europe's deepest and oldest lakes.

The Shkumbin and Mat rivers are central Albania's main waterways. These rivers often run dry in the summer. During heavy winter rains, the rivers become torrents. Their channels sometimes change course. The Mat River has one hydroelectric dam. It creates a reservoir called Lake Ulzës.

The Vjosë River begins in Greece and runs northwestward across the Albanian border. The river passes a series of narrow gorges. It forms the southern edge of the Myzeqe Plain. South of the Vjosë, its tributary the Drino River travels through a wide valley. The Drino passes the ancient town of Gjirokastër on its way to the Strait of Otranto.

Three large freshwater lakes lie along Albania's eastern edge. Lake Ohrid straddles the Albania-Macedonia border. The lake's clear, spring-fed water is transparent to a depth of 70 feet (21 m). Lake Prespa and Little Lake Prespa lie just southeast of Lake Ohrid. The borders of Macedonia, Albania, and Greece meet in the middle of Lake Prespa. Little Lake Prespa straddles the Albania-Greece border.

▶ Climate

Albania has a varied climate. Warm, moist breezes blow eastward from the sea. Colder, drier winds blow westward from the mountains. In general, the coastal lowlands have higher temperatures and lower rainfall. The highlands have lower temperatures and higher rainfall overall. In the early 2000s, several droughts have struck Albania. These times of little or no rain caused crops to fail and rivers to run dry.

Along the Albanian coast, summer temperatures can top 100°F (38°C). The average coastal temperature in July, the hottest month, is 75°F (24°C). Winter brings sudden, heavy thunderstorms. The bora is a cold, strong wind that blows from the north or northeast. It lowers temperatures to an

average of 44°F (7°C) in January, the coldest month. Albania's high mountains prevent severe winter weather from reaching the coast.

Albanians who live in the mountains experience temperatures around 32°F (0°C) in midwinter. Heavy rains fall between September and May. The average annual precipitation (rain and snow) exceeds 100 inches (254 centimeters) in the North Albanian Alps. Snow covers the highest peaks for much of the year. Farther south, however, the weather is milder. Temperatures are warmer, and precipitation is lighter. During the summer months, mountain nights are cool. Temperatures may drop to about 40°F (4°C). Daytime summer temperatures in the highlands average about 66°F (19°C).

◉ Flora and Fauna

Albania's plains, mountains, and waters support a variety of plants and animals. Maquis, a type of evergreen shrubland, covers most of the lowlands. Drought-resistant plants such as sage, juniper, and myrtle are common here.

The golden eagle is Albania's national symbol. Albanians call their land Shqipëria, which means "the country of eagles."

Forests cover about 36 percent of Albania. Some woods exist in the lowlands, but most of Albania's forest lies above 3,000 feet (914 m). Large stands of oak, beech, elm, and other deciduous (leaf-shedding) trees begin here. At higher elevations, black pines, fir trees, and other conifers (cone-bearing evergreen trees) are common. So are shrubs and small trees such as oleander, pomegranate, and chaste trees. Above about 5,900 feet (1,800 m), trees and shrubs give way to alpine grasslands.

Wild birds are plentiful in Albania. Ducks, swans, herons, pelicans, and cormorants live in the coastal marshes. Partridges, pheasants, and capercaillies (a type of large grouse) wander the forests. Vultures and golden eagles soar over the mountains.

Albania's highlands are home to many mammals. Hares, foxes, wild boars, wild goats, chamois (small, goat-like antelopes), and deer are fairly common. A few endangered mammals, such as brown bears, gray wolves, and lynx, also survive in remote areas.

Dolphins and sturgeon are common species swimming along the seacoast. So are several varieties of rays, as well as jellyfish colonies that arrive in warm weather and pose a danger to swimmers. Sea turtles migrate up and down the coast too, coming ashore to lay their eggs. Common freshwater species in Albania include trout, carp, and mullet.

Albania is home to one of Europe's last wolf populations. These wolves, called *ujku* in Albanian, live in the remote forests of eastern and northern Albania. Hunting has taken a heavy toll on them. About 250 wolves survive in Albania.

Natural Resources

Albania has a variety of mineral resources. Valuable chromite deposits lie near the Drin River. (Processed chromite is a key ingredient in stainless steel.) This ore is an important Albanian export. The highlands also have deposits of copper, iron ore, nickel, limestone, bitumen, and asphalt. Albanians use the last two materials in road construction.

Albania's energy industry draws on other resources. Lignite, a soft brown coal, provides fuel for some Albanian power plants. The rushing waters of the Drin and Mat rivers power hydroelectric plants. Albania exports some of this energy to neighboring countries. Albania claims ownership of several offshore oil fields. The government has signed agreements with foreign companies to extract this valuable fuel. Albania also plans to tap its underground reserves of natural gas.

Albania's land and water are key natural resources too. Lowland Albanian farms benefit from a mild climate. Albania's many rivers supply ample water for irrigation and fish farming. The nearby seas teem with fish and shellfish. Albania's forests supply wood for fuel and construction.

Environmental Issues

Political and economic struggles during the 1900s and early 2000s have damaged Albania's natural environment. Poverty makes it hard for ordinary Albanians to survive without harming the environment. Meanwhile, political turmoil weakens the government's ability to make and enforce environmental laws.

Albania lacks a nationwide system to distribute electricity. So many households burn wood for cooking and heating. This causes rapid deforestation, or loss of trees. Deforestation harms Albania's wildlife by destroying habitat. Hunting, too, endangers birds and mammals, while overfishing depletes many rivers.

Coastal Albania lies directly over a fault, or fracture in Earth's crust. As a result, Albania sometimes experiences earthquakes.

In hilly regions, Albanians practice terrace farming. Farmers dig small, level terraces into hillsides to raise crops. Terrace farming and deforestation cause heavy erosion (washing away of soil) when it rains. A small reforestation project is under way, but Albania continues to cut trees faster than it replaces them.

Albania's cities are growing fast. Sanitation (sewage and garbage removal) is inadequate in most cities. Garbage landfills are overflowing. Wastewater from homes and factories often goes directly into rivers. Polluted water finds its way into the sea. The water can sicken people as well as fish and waterfowl. Coal- and wood-burning heaters, as well as mining and industry, dump toxic gases into Albania's air. Cars and buses belch dirty clouds of exhaust. Heavy construction also produces dust and dangerous debris.

Many Albanian factories, such as this one in Elbasan, have taken steps to decrease pollution. They have replaced outdated equipment and installed filters that block harmful gases from escaping into the atmosphere.

Mount Dajti overlooks **the capital city of Tiranë.** Tiranë became Albania's capital in 1920.

◉ Cities

TIRANË (population 727,000) is Albania's capital and largest city. It lies 50 miles (80 km) from the coast in north central Albania. Mount Dajti and other peaks rise near the city. Main highways leading north, south, and east from Tiranë link the coastal lowlands to the Central Highlands.

The Ottoman general Süleyman Pasha Mulleti founded Tiranë in 1614. The Turks built public baths, shops, and a mosque (a house of worship for Muslims, followers of Islam) in the city. It remained a quiet outpost of the Ottoman Empire until the early 1900s, when Albania declared its independence. In 1920 Albanian officials named Tiranë the nation's capital. After World War II, Tiranë grew rapidly and became Albania's key manufacturing center. Factories there make foodstuffs, textiles (cloth goods), and heavy machinery.

Tiranë boasts a national art gallery, Albania's oldest and largest university, and a large public park. Government offices line the Avenue of the Martyrs. Skanderbeg Square, a popular plaza, is named after a hero of Albania's long struggle against Ottoman rule.

 Visit www.vgsbooks.com for links to websites with additional information about Albania's capital and other cities.

In Durrës modern houses complete with satellite dishes overlook the ruins of an ancient Roman amphitheater.

DURRËS (population 246,000) is Albania's second-largest city and its leading port. The Greeks founded Durrës in the 600s B.C. In the 100s B.C., the ancient Romans made Durrës the western end point of the Via Egnatia. This important road linked the Adriatic Sea to the distant city of Constantinople (modern Istanbul, Turkey). In Durrës the Romans also built an amphitheater (outdoor theater) that could seat twenty thousand spectators. After Albania declared independence from the Ottoman Empire, Durrës served as the capital from 1914 until 1920.

Modern Durrës is an important commercial port. It links Albania to ports in Italy, Greece, and Montenegro. The city is also a hub of Albania's small railway system. Factories there produce televisions, radios, cigarettes, tractors, and wine. Aleksander Moisiu University opened its doors to students in 2006.

VLORË (population 124,000) is a port on the wide Bay of Vlorë in southern Albania. Founded by the ancient Greeks, Vlorë was the site of Albania's declaration of independence in 1912. Many of the nation's exports and imports pass through this city, which lies just across the Strait of Otranto from Italy. To promote tourism, the government encourages resort development along the coast south of Vlorë.

SHKODËR (population 110,000) is the largest city in northern Albania. It was the capital of the Illyrian Empire. The imposing Fortress of Rozafa overlooks Shkodër from a rocky outcropping. Illyrians, Romans, Venetians, and Ottoman Turks have occupied the fortress. Shkodër residents rebuilt many of the city's buildings after a strong earthquake in 1979. Shkodër is an important cultural and industrial center. It is home to a university and several museums and theaters. The city produces mechanical and electrical components, textiles, and food products. Nearby Lake Shkodër attracts summer tourists.

GJIROKASTËR (population 35,000) is a town in southern Albania. Its architecture contrasts sharply with the factories and drab concrete apartments of Albania's larger cities. Cobblestone streets wind among Gjirokastër's tall, whitewashed houses with red tile roofs. Many of these homes are centuries old. The city first developed around a hilltop fortress in the A.D. 1100s. It was a center of armed resistance to Ottoman rule in the 1800s. In 1961 the government banned new construction in the town, making Gjirokastër a "museum city." The town is also famous as the birthplace of the Communist leader Enver Hoxha.

Quaint and historic **Gjirokastër** is one of the few surviving Ottoman merchant towns in the Balkan region.

HISTORY AND GOVERNMENT

Archaeologists have discovered pottery fragments indicating that Albania has been inhabited for at least five thousand years. As early as 2000 B.C., Greek-speaking peoples were moving south through the Balkan Peninsula. Settlements near the Adriatic Sea traded with ports to the south (modern Greece).

Illyrian civilization took shape on the Balkan Peninsula about 1000 B.C. The Illyrians, a group of independent tribes with a shared culture, built self-governing cities throughout the western Balkan region. They traded with other Balkan peoples. They also had contact with cities on the Italian Peninsula.

In the 600s B.C., Greeks from the nearby island of Corfu began building settlements and trading ports on the Illyrian coast. Greek communities thrived at Apollonia (near modern Vlorë) and Epidamnos (modern Durrës). The Illyrians resisted Greek colonization. Illyrian raiders seized Greek trading ships and attacked the coastal cities. The Greek settlements were valuable prizes for the Illyrian chieftains.

◉ Illyria and Rome

Several Illyrian chieftains united their tribes into kingdoms. In the 380s B.C., Illyrian king Bardyllis fought with Greek settlers in Epirus, in the Illyrian-Greek border region. Another Illyrian king, Glaucias, wrested Epidamnos from the Greeks in 312 B.C. Glaucias then allied with Rome, a nation that was gaining control of the Italian Peninsula.

In the 200s B.C., the Illyrian king Agron united many independent cities. He greatly expanded Illyrian territory. Agron made Shkodër his capital. He built an army and navy to protect Illyrian cities.

After Agron's death in 230 B.C., rule of Illyria passed to his widow, Teuta. She ordered attacks on Greek coastal cities. She also authorized Illyrian piracy in the Adriatic Sea. The latter act angered Rome. Rome sent ambassadors to negotiate with the Illyrians. One of them insulted Teuta, and her attendants murdered him. Rome invaded Illyria in revenge. The Romans defeated Teuta's army and seized the port of Epidamnos. They renamed it Dyrrachium.

In 168 B.C., Illyria became the Roman province of Illyricum. During the Roman era, outsiders began calling Illyrians the Albani, after the name of one Illyrian tribe. The name later came to include other Illyrian tribes.

Roman engineers extended an old Illyrian road and named it Via Egnatia. The 696-mile (1,120 km) road ran from Dyrrachium to Byzantium (modern Istanbul, Turkey). The road became a vital trade route. It also helped the Roman army control the Balkan Peninsula.

By the A.D. 100s, the Roman Empire was immense. It covered much of Europe, all of Asia Minor, and the eastern and southern Mediterranean coasts. Rome needed a strong military to repel raids from northern Europe. The Roman army enlisted many Illyrian soldiers. They were famous for their skill and discipline.

Christianity was spreading from the Roman province of Palestine (modern Israel) throughout the empire. For three centuries, the Roman government persecuted Christians. It believed Christianity threatened the empire's stability. Nonetheless, many Illyrians—and other residents of the empire—accepted Christianity.

Emperor Constantine

Several Illyrians, including Emperor Constantine I, rose through the political ranks to become Roman emperors. In the 300s, Constantine adopted Christianity and made it the empire's official religion. He also moved the capital from the city of Rome on the Italian Peninsula to Constantinople (formerly Byzantium).

Despite Rome's strength, many Illyrian tribes resisted Roman rule. They also repelled invasions by northern European peoples. The tribes living in the rugged and inaccessible mountains held fast to their ancient customs, religion, and independence. By and large, Roman authority could not reach them.

Byzantine Rule

Raids by northern peoples continued through the 300s. The Roman army suffered a series of defeats. The empire gradually lost control of its provinces. It was proving too large to control or protect from one capital.

When Emperor Theodosius I died in 395, his sons Arcadius and Honorius divided the empire into western and eastern halves. Honorius ruled from Rome, while Arcadius ruled from Constantinople. Northern Illyria remained under Roman influence. Southern Illyria forged closer links with Constantinople.

The Western Roman Empire collapsed in the 400s. The Eastern

Roman Empire, or Byzantine Empire, survived. Byzantine emperors ruled Illyria. Byzantine armies fought invaders from the north for control of the Balkan Peninsula.

Medieval Albania

In the 500s, the Slavs of eastern Europe invaded the Balkan Peninsula. The Slavs intermarried with many local peoples. They introduced their language and culture to the region.

But the ancient Illyrian communities remained independent. By this time, Illyrians had begun calling themselves Albanians. Albanian landowning families ruled over large private domains. Along the coast, strong dynasties (ruling families) governed the ports. In the mountains, Albanian clans (family alliances) fought over territory and scarce natural resources.

Meanwhile, the Bulgars moved into Europe from central Asia. In the 800s, they founded the Bulgarian Empire. Bulgarian leader Simeon I defeated the Byzantine army and expanded his empire. It covered most of the Balkan Peninsula, including Albania.

But the Byzantine emperor Basil II, also called Basil the Bulgar Slayer, counterattacked in 1014. Byzantine forces smashed the Bulgarian army. They regained not only the Balkan Peninsula but also southern Italy. However, because these territories lay far from Constantinople, Byzantine authority there gradually weakened.

Basil II (958–1025) led the Byzantine Empire through many years of war and prosperity during his reign from 976 to 1025. This image is a reproduction of an eleventh-century manuscript.

Meanwhile, Christianity was going through important changes. Christian leaders in Rome and Constantinople disagreed over proper beliefs and practices. This disagreement—added to centuries of geographic separation, language differences, and political turmoil—led to the Great Schism in 1054. This was a split of the Christian Church. Constantinople became the center of the Eastern Orthodox Church. Rome became the headquarters of the Roman Catholic Church.

The boundary between the two Christian domains followed the Shkumbin River. It split Albanians into two distinct cultural groups. Most Ghegs of northern Albania adopted Roman Catholicism. Most Tosks of southern Albania adopted Eastern Orthodox Christianity.

Albanian clans, struggling with one another over land and divided by religion, could not prevent further foreign occupation. Albanian ports were valuable prizes for outsiders. Normans invading from southern Italy conquered Durrës in 1081. In 1202 Durrës passed to Venice, a wealthy merchant state on the northern Adriatic Sea. Venetians built trading posts throughout Albania's lowlands.

In 1272 Charles d'Anjou, king of Naples and Sicily in southern Italy, attacked. He conquered Durrës and much of central Albania. He called his new domain the Kingdom of Albania.

Meanwhile, the Serbs to the northeast had occupied northern and eastern Albania and established a dynasty at Shkodër. In the early 1300s, the Serbian king Stefan Dusan conquered the western half of the Balkan Peninsula. He crowned himself emperor of the Serbs, Greeks, Bulgarians, and Albanians and drew up a legal code for his subjects.

Charles I (Charles d'Anjou) conquered Albania in 1272.

But in 1355, while leading an attack on Constantinople, Dusan suddenly died. His empire crumbled.

The constant warfare in Albania caused poverty and famine (severe food shortages). Many Albanians left their troubled homeland and settled in Greece or southern Italy.

◉ Turkish Conquest

The chaos allowed several Albanian clans to establish powerful domains. For example, the Balsic dynasty took control of Shkodër and the northern highlands. The cities of Durrës and Cërujë fell to the Kastrioti dynasty. The Dukagjini family ruled Lezhë. Conflict among these dynasties soon led to civil war. The fighting weakened Albania's defenses.

Meanwhile, the powerful Ottoman Empire was expanding from Turkey onto the Balkan Peninsula. In 1389 the Turks defeated the Serbs at the Battle of Kosovo, northeast of Albania. This event ended Serbian power on the Balkan Peninsula.

In the early 1400s, the Turks conquered Epirus. They moved north into Albania. The squabbling Albanian dynasties could not unite. The Turks quickly overran Albania.

To govern this region, the Turks offered Albanian landowners the opportunity to become pashas (governors) of pashalics (Ottoman provinces). Pashas had to pledge their loyalty to the Ottoman sultan, or king.

One of many clan leaders who accepted this offer was Gjon Kastrioti. To ensure his loyalty, the Turks took his son Gjergj Kastrioti to live at the sultan's court. There, young Kastrioti received military training and Islamic instruction.

Gjergj Kastrioti became a high-ranking officer in the Ottoman army. He led Turkish forces to many victories. To honor his military skill, the Turks gave Kastrioti the name Iskander Bey (Lord Alexander). It compared him to the ancient Greek king Alexander the Great. Albanians translated the name as Skanderbeg.

In 1443 Skanderbeg led a Turkish army at the Battle of Nis

THE CANON OF LEKË DUKAGJINI

Turkish control did not reach into the rugged highlands. Here many Albanian clans preserved their laws and independence.

The Canon of Lekë Dukagjini is a legal code named for an Albanian prince of the 1400s. It governed everything from how to treat strangers and arrange marriages to how to pay taxes and settle property disputes.

The code has governed Albanian society—especially in the highlands—for hundreds of years. Clan elders use it to resolve disputes and punish wrongdoing. It still governs many social customs in modern Albania.

in Serbia. During the battle, he switched sides with a few hundred Albanian Ottoman soldiers. Afterward, he trekked to Cërujë, captured its castle, and abandoned Islam and the Ottoman Empire. He mustered thousands of Albanian soldiers and built many fortresses. He organized a league of Albanian princes to fight for independence. This force turned back more than a dozen Turkish invasions over two decades.

Skanderbeg fell ill and died in 1468. The Turks attacked Albania again. This time they won. By 1500 only the most isolated highlands of Albania remained free of Turkish control. The Turks forcibly converted most Albanians to Islam.

Ottoman Rule

After their victory, the Turks imposed heavy taxes on Albanians. They seized property from those who would not convert to Islam. They forbade Christians from holding government jobs.

About two-thirds of Albanians became Muslims. Many did so in order to join the Turkish civil service (government workforce). Only Muslims could become pashas. Throughout the 1500s and 1600s, the Albanian pashas often fought among themselves. This kept them from cooperating in a rebellion against the Turks. Some Albanians became soldiers and officers in the Turkish army. Others became pashas of Ottoman territories outside Albania.

By the late 1700s, the Ottoman Empire was in decline. The Turkish administration grew inefficient and corrupt. Opponents began fighting for Ottoman territory. The most powerful landowning families in Albania held more authority there than the sultan did. Mehmed Pasha Bushati controlled the pashalic of Shkodër in northern Albania. Ahmet Kurt Pasha ruled the pashalic of Berat in central Albania. Ali Pasha governed the pashalic of Ioánnina in southern Albania.

The capital of Ioánnina became an important commercial, political, and cultural center. Its economy thrived on trade with Italy. The city was home to many excellent schools. It produced and attracted famous scholars and writers. Great Britain and France sent diplomats to live in Ioánnina.

Ali Pasha's power made the sultan jealous and fearful. He ordered the Turks to attack Ioánnina in 1820. Two years later, they captured and killed Ali Pasha. But he had inspired rebellion against Ottoman rule in both Albania and Greece.

Independence

In the mid-1800s, Turkish officials created a new legal system. It divided the Albanian-populated lands into four vilayets (provinces)—Shkodër, Kosovo, Monastir, and Ioánnina—and increased the sultan's authority throughout the empire. But the Balkan peoples opposed these changes. Revolt swept through the region.

Other nations saw this unrest as a chance to expand their power. Russia wanted ports and allies in southern Europe. The British wanted to seize Turkish territory and to stop Russian expansion. Italy and Austria wanted strategic towns and forts on the Adriatic coast.

In 1878 Russia defeated Ottoman forces on the Balkan Peninsula. Russia, Turkey, and several European nations signed treaties granting independence to some Balkan states. The treaties turned over territories with large Albanian populations to Montenegro, Serbia, and Bulgaria. Albania remained part of the Ottoman Empire.

In the same year, Albanian leaders formed the League of Prizren. The league vowed to fight the designs of stronger European powers. It also sought more freedom for Albanians living under Ottoman rule.

At first Turkey supported the league. Ottoman leaders hoped it would help stop Austria and Italy from seizing Balkan land. But when Albanian forces won back territory from Montenegro, the sultan began to fear

Russian and Turkish leaders gather to sign the Treaty of San Stefano in 1878. The treaty freed several Balkan countries from Ottoman control, but Albania was not one of them.

THE EAGLE OF ALBANIA

The eagle has been a symbol of Albania for many centuries. It appeared in the emblems of powerful ancient families, such as the Kastrioti emblem. Skanderbeg's forces carried a flag with a black, two-headed eagle while fighting the Ottoman Turks. This sign also rallied Albanians to fight for independence in the early 1900s.

them. In 1881 his army attacked and defeated them. The league broke up.

Turkey was determined to keep control of Albania. To achieve this goal, Ottoman officials banned Albanian writings, public schooling, and the Albanian language. Many Albanians emigrated (moved from Albania to other nations) in search of education and jobs.

But the Ottoman Empire continued to weaken, and the Albanian drive for freedom survived. Albanian nationalists (people who wanted an independent Albania) published their writings abroad. They sought support in Europe and in the United States. They also found allies within the Turkish government.

In 1909 Albanians serving in the Ottoman army revolted. Albanian independence fighters attacked Turkish forces in Shkodër and Kosovo. In 1911 rebels forced the Turks to retreat from Albania's northern highlands.

Turkey could not stem the revolt. It granted self-rule to the four Albanian vilayets. On November 28, 1912, Albanian leaders declared their country's independence. Ismail Qemali headed the new Albanian government.

Turmoil in the Balkans

At the same time, war broke out on the Balkan Peninsula. The region became a confusing battleground of states and ethnic groups competing for land. The Albanians could not agree on a common path for their young nation.

Stronger European states wanted to settle these conflicts. In 1913 European leaders recognized Albanian independence. They drew up a new Albanian constitution. The document defined the nation's basic principles and laws. It stated that elected lawmakers would share power with a monarch (a king or queen). The European leaders chose the German prince Wilhelm zu Wied as the first monarch. Then they drew Albania's border. The border left large Albanian communities outside the country, in Montenegro, Kosovo, Macedonia, and northern Greece.

The poorly organized Albanians had little say in these decisions. As a result, independence did not bring peace to Albania. Rival clans clashed over territory. Landowners jockeyed for influence in the new government.

Prince Wilhelm arrived in the capital city, Durrës, in March 1914. Albanian politician Essad Pasha denounced the prince as a puppet of foreign nations and formed a rebel army.

World War I

Opposition to Prince Wilhelm grew quickly among the Albanians. Six months after taking office, he fled.

Meanwhile, in summer 1914, a Bosnian Serb murdered the heir to the throne of Austria-Hungary. This empire had recently conquered all or part of several Balkan nations. Some Balkan nationalists hoped to gain independence for the conquered peoples by starting a war with Austria-Hungary.

Austria-Hungary declared war on Serbia, which had backed the assassination. Previous treaties soon brought Germany, Bulgaria, and the Ottoman Empire to Austria-Hungary's aid. This group was called the Central powers. Likewise, Russia, the United Kingdom, France, Italy, the United States, and other nations joined Serbia. This group was called the Allied powers, or Allies. Thus, in fall 1914, World War I began.

During World War I, several nations battled for control of Albania. Greece attacked in the south. Italy occupied Vlorë. France took control of the Korçë Basin. Austria-Hungary, Montenegro, Bulgaria, and Serbia also marched into Albania. Albanians, leaderless and divided by clan and religion, were too weak to prevent any of this.

World War I ended in November 1918. Representatives of the victorious Allies met in Paris, France, to redraw the map of Europe. They agreed—without Albanian consent—to divide Albania among Greece, Italy, and Yugoslavia. Yugoslavia was a nation created in 1918. It included modern Slovenia, Croatia, Bosnia and Herzegovina, Serbia, Kosovo, and Macedonia.

Albanian leaders rejected the plan. They held a conference at Lushnjë in January 1920. They again declared Albania's independence,

During World War I, **Italian engineering troops raise a small bridge** to assist the movement of Allied forces through Albania.

warning that Albanians would take up arms to defend it. They named Tiranë as the new capital. The United States supported Albania and blocked the Paris agreement.

King Zog

After the war, Albanian liberals wanted change. They struggled to establish a modern government and to reform the ancient landowner-ship system. Then a conservative faction emerged. The conservatives fought against change in Albania.

Ahmed Zogu, a politician and landowner, led the conservatives. In 1922 he became prime minister, or head of the Albanian government.

In June 1924, conservative supporters murdered a liberal leader. Liberal supporters revolted. Zogu fled to Yugoslavia. Fan Noli, an Eastern Orthodox bishop (church leader) and liberal legislator, orga-nized a new Albanian administration.

Noli sought to reform Albania's economy. But he couldn't attract foreign aid. Conservatives strongly opposed him. By late 1924, conflict had paralyzed the Albanian legislature. In December Zogu returned with an army of Yugoslav soldiers and overthrew Noli.

Zogu declared himself president of Albania in 1925. He took over many of the legislature's powers. He signed several military, economic, and political agreements with Italy. These agreements gave Italy great influence over Albania while protecting Albania from invasion.

In 1928 Zogu dissolved the legislature and created a monarchy. He named himself King Zog I and held nearly complete power.

Liberal Albanians take part in an armed revolt against conservative Albanians in June 1924. The two groups disagreed about the modernization of Albania.

The king planned to modernize Albania's economy. The government broke up some large private estates. It set up a bank to help farmers. King Zog also ordered the construction of new roads, port facilities, and industries.

But the alliance with Italy soon brought trouble. Italian ruler Benito Mussolini wanted to make Albania a colony dependent on Italy. He demanded that Albania establish Italian communities. He wanted Albanian schools to teach Italian.

Albanians protested. They feared an Italian takeover. The king's tight grip on power inspired an opposition movement of Albanian Communists. The Communists worked secretly to overthrow King Zog and return power to the Albanian people.

World War II

Events elsewhere in Europe were leading to another world war. Nazi leader Adolf Hitler took power in Germany. He strengthened Germany's military. He allied with Mussolini. Germany and Italy aimed to conquer all of Europe. They began taking over neighboring countries.

In April 1939, Italian troops attacked Albania. Mussolini wanted to make King Zog a puppet of Italy's government. Rather than accept Italian control, Zog fled to Greece. Italy occupied Tiranë and took over Albania.

Five months later, Germany invaded Poland. This touched off World War II. The Axis powers (Germany, Italy, Japan, and their allies) fought on one side. On the other side fought the Allied powers (France, the United Kingdom, and later the United States, and their allies).

Mussolini ordered an attack on northern Greece in fall 1940. The Greeks repelled it. Greek and Yugoslavian troops then marched into Albania to fight the Italians. In spring 1941, Germany came to Italy's aid. The German army attacked Albania and Greece.

Albanians formed resistance groups to harass the German and Italian forces. Meanwhile, Albanian Communists formed a political party led by Hoxha. Communist resistance fighters and members of non-Communist resistance groups joined forces.

Mussolini fell from power in 1943. Italy soon withdrew from Albania. After a series of fierce battles, the Germans retreated in November 1944. Albanian resistance groups began fighting one another. This internal conflict worsened the war's destruction. World War II ended in 1945. It had destroyed nearly one-third of Albania's housing, livestock, and farms.

Communist Albania

With support from Yugoslavia's Communist Party, Hoxha established a provisional (temporary) Albanian government. Communist candidates easily defeated their opponents in Albania's first postwar elections in late 1945.

Hoxha renamed his country the People's Republic of Albania. The nation's Communist Party became the only legal political organization. Hoxha cut off trade and diplomatic relations with Western Europe. He allied Albania closely with Joseph Stalin, the brutal leader of the Soviet Union (a Communist nation composed of Russia and fourteen other republics).

Albania's rulers followed Stalin's example. Hoxha and his right-hand man, Mehmet Shehu, changed Albania into a strict Socialist state. (In a Socialist state, groups of workers or the nation as a whole—not individuals—own the nation's resources and its means of production.) The government seized property and land. It executed or imprisoned opponents. The state became the sole employer. Private ownership of farms, factories, mines, shops, and other businesses—as well as homes and automobiles—became illegal.

Hoxha used Soviet financial aid to improve Albania's schools, hospitals, and transportation system. Albania quickly built new industries. Soon nearly half the population worked in manufacturing, mining, or construction.

Albania also entered a close economic partnership with Yugoslavia. But some Albanians complained about Yugoslav influence in Albania. Meanwhile, Yugoslav-Soviet relations went sour. In the late 1940s, Albania and Yugoslavia broke off relations.

In the 1950s, Albania joined the Warsaw Pact. The Soviet Union led this military alliance of Communist nations. To help Albania's economy, Soviet leaders sent advisers, equipment, and financial aid. New Albanian factories assembled products for export to other Warsaw Pact countries.

Isolation

In 1953 Stalin died. Many Albanians called for changes in Albania's Stalinist system. But the system kept power in Hoxha's hands, so he resisted these demands. He criticized Nikita Khrushchev, Stalin's successor. Hoxha ordered the arrest of Albanians who supported Khrushchev's reforms.

In 1961 the Soviet Union and China—the world's two largest Communist nations—disagreed over economic and foreign policies. The Chinese leader Mao Zedong, like Hoxha, opposed Khrushchev's reforms. Albania publicly supported China in this dispute.

Khrushchev broke off relations with Albania. Soviet leaders halted economic aid and withdrew Soviet-supplied equipment. This left Albanian factories without machinery, raw materials, or spare parts.

To stop an economic crash, Albania allied with China. The Chinese sent equipment and advisers to help Albanian industries.

In 1968 the Soviet Union invaded Czechoslovakia (modern Czech Republic and Slovakia) to halt a reform movement there. Fearing an invasion of Albania, Hoxha withdrew his country from the Warsaw Pact. He also cracked down on Albanian opposition. His secret police imprisoned thousands of people suspected of disloyalty. Hoxha's regime also announced that Albania would become an atheist state (one without religion). Security forces arrested Muslim and Christian clergy. The government banned public worship and closed all churches and mosques.

In the early 1970s, China opened diplomatic relations with the United States. (U.S.-China relations had been frozen for more than twenty years.) Hoxha saw the United States as a dangerous enemy. He cut ties with the Chinese government. In 1978 China stopped all military and financial aid to Albania. Albania had no allies left.

Hoxha wanted Albania to be completely independent. The government outlawed traveling abroad, reading foreign publications, and listening to foreign radio broadcasts. No visitors could enter Albania. The regime banned trade with non-Communist nations. Hoxha feared a European or U.S. invasion. He ordered the construction of more than eight hundred thousand concrete military bunkers in the countryside.

Albanian Communist leader Enver Hoxha votes in—and wins—the nation's 1967 election. He ruled until his death in 1985.

Albania's trade restrictions destroyed its economy. Hoxha's harsh policies also sparked opposition within his own government. In 1981 Mehmet Shehu called for opening foreign trade with non-Communist nations. Hoxha rebuked Shehu and tried to convince him to step down. Shehu refused. In December 1981, Shehu died of a bullet wound to the head. The government called the death a suicide. But many Albanians believed that Hoxha had Shehu murdered. Afterward, the secret police arrested and killed government officials who supported Shehu's views.

Rejoining Europe

In the early 1980s, Hoxha's health began to fail. He named Ramiz Alia, a close friend and political ally, as his successor. Hoxha died in April 1985. Alia took over. Under Alia, Albania gradually opened up its economic policies and established diplomatic ties with more than one hundred countries.

Nevertheless, factory production fell and Albania continued its slide into economic depression. The ban on travel and on reading foreign publications continued. Thousands of political prisoners remained under arrest. With their living standard rapidly deteriorating, many Albanians demanded change.

In 1989 widespread economic failure sparked public demonstrations in Europe's other Communist nations. For the first time since World War II, Warsaw Pact countries held free elections. Some of these elections ousted Soviet-allied Communist governments. In addition, some of the republics that made up Yugoslavia declared independence. This caused civil war and chaos along Albania's northern and eastern borders through the 1990s.

Alia eased travel restrictions and allowed citizens to own private homes. He freed most political prisoners, gave state-owned businesses some independence, and lifted the ban on religion. Albania also sought financial aid from non-Communist nations.

But these measures could not stem the rising tide of opposition to Albania's Communist government. Violent antigovernment demonstrations broke out in Shkodër. A mob in Tiranë destroyed a huge statue of Hoxha.

Conditions in Albania worsened, and demonstrations turned into ever more violent conflicts. In 1990 thousands of Albanians stormed foreign embassies in Tiranë to seek asylum (protection) abroad. Many others fled to Greece and Italy. To stop the violence, the Communist Party legalized opposition parties and called for open elections. The government renamed the country the Republic of Albania and drew up a new constitution. This document established an elected presidency.

In 1991 the Soviet Union fell apart. In Albania the Democratic Party (Partia Demokratike, or PD)—the largest party opposing the

Demonstrators knock down a statue of Hoxha during a pro-democracy rally in Tiranë in 1991.

Communists—rallied thousands of students, farmers, and towns-people to its ranks. In 1992, after winning a majority of seats in the Albanian legislature, the PD took power. The PD-dominated legislature elected Sali Berisha as Albania's president.

Berisha's government lifted all travel and trade restrictions. The government sold its factories and mining operations. Albanians began growing crops on private farms and selling their harvest on the open market. Albania's new government sought to end its long isolation. In 1994 Albania began the long process of applying to join the North Atlantic Treaty Organization.

The economy continued to struggle, however. Many Albanians emigrated from Albania to Italy in search of jobs. From 1994 to 1996, Albanians across the country invested their life savings in a shaky financial scheme the government had approved. At this time, the government actually had little control over Albania's financial system. Promising good returns, several private companies accepted about $1 billion in deposits from Albanian customers. But the companies had lied about the returns, and the scheme collapsed in 1997. This led to widespread rioting. About two thousand Albanians died. Albania's government nearly collapsed.

The PD lost power after this disaster. In 1997 the Socialist Party (Partia Socialiste, or PS) won Albania's legislative elections, bringing Rexhep Meidani to the presidency.

Meanwhile, conflict in Yugoslavia raged on. At this time, Yugoslavia consisted of Montenegro and Serbia. Kosovo was part of Serbia. But Kosovo's population was about 90 percent Albanian and Muslim, while the rest of Serbia's population was primarily Serbian and Christian. Relations between the two groups were poor and quickly deteriorated into violence.

NATO believed that the Yugoslav government was conducting mass killings of Albanian Kosovars. From March to June 1999, NATO forces

Refugees from the 1999 war in Kosovo walk across the Albanian border to safety.

bombed Yugoslavia. Nearly five hundred thousand Albanian Kosovar refugees spilled over the border into Albania, straining Albania's fragile government and economy. Eventually the Serbian military left Kosovo, along with most Serbian Kosovars. But Kosovo remained officially part of Serbia. The United Nations, an international organization, took over the administration of Kosovo in June 1999.

Alfred Moisiu, a politically neutral candidate, was elected president of Albania in 2002. Bamir Topi of the PD became president in 2007. Albania made progress toward economic and political stability. However, the nation faced several ongoing challenges, including crime and government corruption as well as conflict over Kosovo's status and Kosovar refugees in Albania.

Bamir Topi

Albanian Kosovars fought for Kosovo's independence from Serbia. Albania supported this cause. Kosovo eventually declared its independence in 2008. Albania was the first nation to officially recognize Kosovo as an independent nation. Albania's unwavering support for Kosovo, a stance shared by NATO, helped Albania finally attain NATO membership in 2009.

That year Albania also applied for membership in the European Union. Meanwhile, the Democratic Party won legislative elections by a very slim margin. Socialist Party legislators demanded an investigation. When refused, they began a monthslong boycott of assembly proceedings. In early 2010, EU officials warned Albania that its legislative problems could jeopardize entry into the EU.

Visit www.vgsbooks.com for links to websites with information about Albania's connection with the war in Kosovo in the 1990s.

Despite the political squabbling, by 2010 the Albanian economy had gradually improved. Foreign countries were making new investments. Fewer workers were emigrating. The country's economic production was growing about 5 percent per year. Albania was also attracting many visitors to its beaches and historic sites. These visitors contributed to a promising new tourism industry. Albania had at last rejoined the international community and world economy.

◉ Government

A constitution passed in 1998 guides Albania's government. The Albanian government is a parliamentary democracy. In this system, the parliament (legislature) chooses the leader of the executive branch. (In Albania, the president and prime minister share this leadership.) The executive branch is responsible for the day-to-day administration of the government.

The Assembly of the Republic of Albania is Albania's legislature. Its 140 members serve four-year terms. The assembly has the power to rewrite the constitution, pass laws, draw up a national budget, and confirm or revoke a presidential declaration of war. Every five years, the legislature elects Albania's president.

The president is Albania's head of state, or chief public representative. The president is responsible for observation of the constitution and enforcement of laws and is commander in chief of the military. The president appoints the prime minister—usually the head of the assembly's majority party. The prime minister is the head of government and leads the council of ministers. These ministers, selected by the president according to the prime minister's recommendations, are the heads of the government's fourteen ministries. The ministries direct the daily activities of government agencies.

Albania's judicial system consists of a Constitutional Court, a Supreme Court, and multiple lower courts. The Constitutional Court judges the constitutionality of new laws and resolves disputes within the government. The legislature elects its members. The Supreme Court is Albania's highest court of appeal. The president appoints its members with the legislature's approval. The lower courts are criminal, civil, or military courts. Albania has no jury trials. In the lower courts, a three-judge panel decides each case.

Albania consists of twelve counties. The counties are further divided into thirty-six districts and 351 municipalities. Many small towns and villages have no government presence. Councils of elders enforce the laws, make important decisions, and dispense justice.

THE PEOPLE

Albania is home to 3.2 million people. The population is growing at 0.6 percent per year. This is one of the highest growth rates in Europe. Among continental European nations, only Kosovo's population is growing faster. However, as Albania continues to lose people through emigration, experts believe its population will begin to shrink. Researchers expect the population to fall to 2.9 million by 2050—a decrease of 9 percent.

Albania's population density is 287 people per square mile (111 people per sq. km). Albania is slightly more crowded than most other Balkan nations. However, it is only about half as crowded as Kosovo.

Since the mid-1900s, the population of Albania has been changing steadily from rural to urban. In 1950 about 80 percent of Albanians lived in rural areas, while 20 percent lived in cities. Sixty years later, only 52 percent of Albanians live in rural areas while 48 percent live in cities.

Ethnic Heritage

About 95 percent of Albania's people are ethnic Albanians. They trace their ancestors, language, and culture back to the ancient Illyrians.

Albanians stand apart from other ethnic groups on the Balkan Peninsula. When Slavs invaded the region, Illyrians in Albania resisted and did not absorb Slavic culture. In addition, Albania stayed independent from Yugoslavia. As a result, Albanians remain more closely related to their ancient Illyrian ancestors than their neighbors do. Albanians speak a language unique in the region.

Ethnic Albanians belong to two distinct groups. The Ghegs live mainly north of the Shkumbin River. Over the centuries, northern Albania's mountainous terrain helped the Ghegs resist foreign rule. The Tosks dwell mainly in the south. They came into closer contact with outsiders. The Tosks absorbed the ideas and customs of several groups of invaders.

Albanian children have fun posing for a photo. They are from the city of Tiranë.

About 3 percent of Albania's people are Greek. Many Greeks inhabit towns near the southern border. The remaining 2 percent of Albanians are Serbian, Macedonian, Bulgarian, Romanian, or Romani (sometimes called Gypsies).

The Romani are an ethnic group who live throughout Europe—usually somewhat apart from mainstream society. Their ancestors began migrating from India to Europe at least one thousand years ago. The Romani still speak their ancient language and maintain unique customs of dress, religion, music, and family life.

Women and Family Life

Albanian women have traditionally held domestic roles, caring for their families and homes. Albanians place great value on childbearing. Many seek to have large families. Albanians typically view having children as the most important duty of wives.

ALBANIANS ABROAD

A 1913 agreement set Albania's modern boundaries. It left half the population of ethnic Albanians in other countries. About two million Albanians live in Macedonia and Montenegro. Another two million Albanians live in Kosovo.

Many Albanian immigrants and their descendants live in southern Italy as well. Albanians have been migrating to Italy since the 1400s. These people call themselves the Arbëreshë. They speak the same dialect (language variety) that Albanians used before the Ottoman conquest of Albania.

Parents often arrange marriages for their sons and daughters. Weddings are festive occasions. An entire village or neighborhood takes part in a lavish meal.

Although the Canon of Lekë Dukagjini is not officially a part of Albanian law, it continues to influence Albanian society. The code prohibits women from inheriting property—and in fact, the code treats women as property. It also prohibits divorce. Due to the code's influence, women in modern Albania have limited ability to work outside the home.

Albania's Communist government encouraged women to enter the workforce. Some rose high in government service. Women also started attending high schools and universities. But the end of Communism brought new challenges. As state-sponsored jobs dwindled, women found their pay shrinking and their job security vanishing. Many left the workforce. Only 46 percent of Albanian women were in the nation's workforce.

This young bride in rural Albania wears a traditional white dress on her wedding day.

An Albanian woman and her two children pose on their family farm. A field of corn and rows of handmade bricks lie beyond them.

THE BLOOD FEUD

The blood feud is a centuries-old Albanian custom. Families and clans may fight for generations over past wrongs. The Canon of Lekë Dukagjini calls for revenge of most wrongs—including murder. Feuds may start over big conflicts, such as physical attacks, or small conflicts, such as property disputes.

Many villages have little policing and no state justice system. As a result, crimes committed in a blood feud receive light punishment—or none at all. An Albanian family may go into hiding to avoid revenge killings after wronging another family. Some Albanian children caught up in blood feuds never leave their homes, even to play with friends or attend school.

Women who can find jobs generally make less money and have less opportunity for advancement than men do. Although Albanian law allows women to own property and obtain loans, many women do not know their rights or do not press for them. In addition, government enforcement of women's rights is weak.

Rural Albanian women are less likely than urban women to pursue education and jobs or to seek political office. Meanwhile, the emigration of men to find work abroad leaves many Albanian women in charge of single-parent households. These women may receive money from husbands and relatives working abroad, but many of these women struggle to pay for food and other necessities.

Albania's traditional clan system survives in Albania's northern highlands. Albanians there seldom move far from home. The typical Albanian clan includes several families. These families share their land and possessions. Clan elders use the Canon of Lekë Dukagjini to settle disputes. Violations of this code sometimes lead to feuding.

◉ Education

Before the 1920s, Albania had no public schools or universities. Its Ottoman rulers forbade teaching in the Albanian language. Only a few private Catholic and Turkish schools operated in the cities.

Many elderly Albanian men are named Wilson. After World War I, U.S. president Woodrow Wilson blocked an agreement that would have divided Albania among Italy, Yugoslavia, and Greece. In Wilson's honor, Albanians named thousands of their newborn sons after him.

Some public schools opened after Albania declared independence in 1912. But nearly 80 percent of the population was illiterate (could not read or write) at the start of World War II.

After World War II, the Communist government made education an important goal. New laws required all children between seven and fifteen years old to attend school. The government built public schools throughout the country. Until the end of Communist rule in the early 1990s, religious instruction was illegal.

In modern Albania, children between three and six years old may attend a *kopshte*, or nursery school. At the age of seven, students begin four years of elementary school. About 95 percent of Albanian children attend elementary school, and 74 percent of Albanian students continue from elementary to a four-year secondary school. Albania's literacy rate is about 99 percent.

Children work in coloring books in a nursery school in Tiranë. This *kopshte* prepares its students to enter elementary school at the age of seven.

College students enjoy coffee and conversation at a rooftop restaurant overlooking Tiranë.

Graduates of secondary schools may continue their studies in colleges or other postsecondary institutes. The University of Tiranë, Albania's first university, opened in 1957. It offers degrees in history, economics, medicine, engineering, and other subjects. By the mid-1990s, several other advanced schools had opened. In 2006 the Aleksander Moisiu University opened in Durrës.

◉ Health

Like Albania's education system, the nation's health-care system improved dramatically after World War II. The government built several hospitals and training colleges for doctors, dentists, and nurses. Since then medical services have been available to Albanians at no charge. The government partially covers the cost of medicines.

Nevertheless, the country's health-care system is outdated. Old equipment slows treatment. Many isolated areas lack clinics and trained health-care workers.

Life expectancy in Albania is seventy-two years for men and seventy-nine years for women. The overall figure, seventy-five years,

Visit www.vgsbooks.com for links to websites with additional information and statistics about education and health care in Albania.

is lower than Greece's life expectancy but average among the other Balkan nations. Albania has one of the highest birthrates in Europe. But the infant mortality rate is also higher than average. In 2009 the number of babies who died before their first birthday stood at 6 per 1,000 births. About 34 of every 1,000 children die before their fifth birthday. Many Albanian women do not get adequate health care during pregnancy and childbirth. As a result, 1 woman in 490 dies from childbearing-related causes.

With its tightly controlled borders and difficult terrain, Albania avoided many communicable diseases for decades—including acquired immunodeficiency syndrome (AIDS), a disease caused by the human immunodeficiency virus (HIV). Albania's HIV infection rate is low. The country reports fewer than one hundred new cases per year. Most of these occur in Tiranë and the coastal cities.

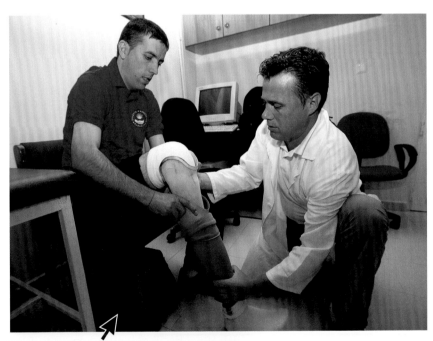

A doctor fits a patient with a prosthetic leg. The patient is from northeastern Albania near the Kosovo border. During the 1999 Kosovo War, combatants littered this region with land mines and other explosives. From 1999 to 2005, 34 people died and 238 were injured when they accidentally touched these devices. With help from the Albanian government and the UN, local residents have successfully de-mined the region.

CULTURAL LIFE

Throughout the late 1900s, Albania's Communist government used culture to win popular support and to control the public. Enver Hoxha's regime enlisted artists and writers to create works glorifying the achievements of workers and farmers under Communist rule.

The government punished people who criticized or made fun of it. Albanian leaders banned Western European styles and frowned on traditional Albanian music and art. Those who did not follow the government's direction had no audience for their works. Some left the country permanently.

These restrictions ended with the fall of Albania's Communist regime. Despite the regime's efforts to the contrary, Albania's long isolation helped preserve its distinct traditional culture. In the twenty-first century, Albanian culture is returning to its roots. It also shows influences from Italy, Turkey, Greece, and the rest of the Balkan region.

● Art

Artists have thrived in Albania despite frequent foreign occupation and warfare over the centuries. Onufri was a painter of the 1500s. He is famous for his icons (Christian religious paintings), which he created during the Ottoman conquest and conversion of many Albanians to Islam. Kolë Idromeno was the most famous artist of the late 1800s and early 1900s, when Albania gained its independence from the Ottoman Empire. He used patriotic themes in many of his paintings.

After independence, the sculptor Odhise Paskali created large sculptures of many Albanian heroes, which are on display in town squares throughout the country. Zef Kolombi studied painting in Rome in the early 1930s. He became famous for his realistic land-scapes, still lifes, and portraits. Vangjush Mio also worked in a realistic style. He created hundreds of paintings and theatrical backdrops from the 1930s through the 1950s. But the Communist regime banned his nude portraits and sketches.

Albanian artists created these statues of Communist leaders Vladimir Lenin, Joseph Stalin, and Enver Hoxha during Albania's Communist era. In 1992 citizens took them down and stored them in an old warehouse.

The arrival of democracy in the early 1990s gave Albanian sculptors and painters greater freedom. Genc Mulliqi specializes in abstract sculpture and paintings. He also directs Albania's national art gallery. Multitalented Ervin Hatibi—a painter, writer, and musician—gained fame as a teenager and has held several exhibitions abroad.

◉ Architecture

Albania's architectural traditions go back to ancient times. The Communist government razed most of the historic buildings in Albania's large towns and cities. However, it did preserve Berat and Gjirokastër as "museum cities." Ancient buildings survive in many other locations too. For example, the Illyrian Fortress of Rozafa still stands near Shkodër. Roman and Greek temples remain in Berat, Byllis, and Durrës. Byzantine churches survive in villages such as Voskopojë. Ottoman mosques survive in Berat and Gjirokastër.

Public buildings in Tiranë reflect a building style imported from Italy in the 1930s. This style is a modern echo of ancient monuments. It was meant to show the grandeur of King Zog's regime.

The traditional Albanian home is made of plastered stone or clay with a red tile roof. Many highland homes are made of wood or unplastered stones. Most city dwellers live in apartments and must guard against burglary and trespassing. Urban apartments have heavy steel doors to prevent unwanted entries.

The Communist regime made a mark on the urban landscape too. Many Albanian city dwellers live in tall concrete apartment blocks. These structures were once a symbol of modernity. But many lack basic services and make uncomfortable dwellings.

In modern Albania, architects are finally free of the bland design of the Communist era, when personal expression was taboo. Several architects have created startling new buildings that ignore past traditions. Albania is drawing attention for the modern architecture and innovative urban planning occurring in Tiranë and other cities. The mayor of Tiranë, Edi Rama, is leading a charge to clean up the capital and to refresh it with new buildings and bright colors. Under his direction, the city has swept away many of the rickety, unsightly structures that once clogged its streets.

Music

Albania has a long, rich tradition of folk music. Musicians in the north are well known for *këngë*, epic songs that recall historical events, fables, dreams, and proverbs. A këngë singer may also play the *lahuta*, a one-stringed fiddle. Throughout Albania music lovers can hear the *gaida*, a type of bagpipe. The gaida is a common instrument at weddings and festivals.

In the south, ensembles called *saze* perform love songs, wedding music, and funeral ballads. Southern Albania is also known for the *kaba*. This is a sad instrumental song led by a clarinet or violin with accompaniment by accordion or *lahutë* (an eight-stringed lute). Remzi

These three boys are dressed in traditional clothing. Two of them play **lahutas,** stringed instruments.

Lela, an Albanian clarinetist, was a leading kaba performer. Lela died in 1995. But the Lela musical dynasty lives on, playing for audiences throughout Europe.

Çesk Zadeja is the father of Albanian classical music. From 1956 until his death in 1997, he composed dozens of works—concertos, symphonies, ballets, and more. He helped found the Music Conservatory of Tiranë, the National Theater of Opera and Ballet, the Assembly of Songs and Dances, and the Academy of Arts. By the mid-1990s, twenty orchestras were performing in Albania. The capital is the site of an annual jazz festival too.

An Albanian rock movement developed outside the country in the 1980s and 1990s. While Albanian bands played in Macedonia and Kosovo, they smuggled recordings of their music into Albania, where rock and roll was against the law. After the fall of Communism, bands such as Troja and Blla Blla Blla gained followings in Albania and worldwide on the Internet. The duo Ritmi i Rrugës (Rhythm of the Street) is a pioneering Albanian rap group. The group is wildly popular on the Balkan Peninsula and performs throughout Europe.

Language

Albanians call their language Shqip. It evolved from the language of the ancient Illyrians. Through contact and conquest, Albanian absorbed some Greek, Latin, Slavic, and Turkish words. Yet Albanian has kept a unique grammar system (structure and rules of usage). Although Albanian belongs to the Indo-European language family—

Posters in Berat, Albania, show written Albanian. This photo, taken in the 1980s, shows political posters, including one with Enver Hoxha's picture on it.

along with nearly all other European languages—Albanian stands alone on its branch of the family tree.

No standard form of written Albanian existed until about a century ago. In 1908 the nation adopted a system of thirty-six letters based on the Latin alphabet. The Latin alphabet is the same one English uses.

Albanian has two distinct dialects: Tosk and Gheg. Tosk and Gheg speakers can understand one another. The official Albanian language uses the Tosk alphabet.

All students in Albanian schools must study other languages. Many Albanians can speak one or two foreign tongues. The most common are English and Italian.

SPEAKING ALBANIAN

Learn a few simple words in the language of Albania.

English	Albanian
Yes	*po* (poh)
No	*jo* (yoh)
Hello	*tungjatjeta* (toong-yah-TYEH-tah)
Good-bye	*mirupafshim* (meer-oo-PAHF-sheem)
Please	*ju lutem* (yoo LOO-tem)
Help	*ndihmë* (n-DEEM)
Thanks	*faleminderit* (fah-leh-meen-DAYR-eet)

⊙ Literature

Albanian literature includes many historical tales and magical myths. These stories pass orally from one generation to the next. Heroic fighters, dragons, witches, snakes, dwarves, and fairies all appear in Albanian folklore. Some Albanians believe in helpful witches called *zana*, who aid those in dire need. The *kukudh* is an ugly dwarf with seven tails. Calling an Albanian a kukudh is a serious insult.

The first prominent Albanian writers were Christian leaders. In 1555 Gjon Buzuku translated the Catholic Church's book of rituals into Albanian. This became the first Albanian-language book. In 1635 Franciscus Blanchus prepared the first Albanian dictionary.

The drive for Albanian independence in the 1800s sparked the Rilindja Kombëtare (National Renaissance). This movement glorified Albanian language and culture within Albanian literature. Rilindja writers used a clear and direct style to celebrate Albania's heroic past. Sami Frashëri, a leader of this movement, penned a history of Albania and the first Albanian stage play. His brother Naim Frashëri authored poetry, histories, and schoolbooks. His epic poem *Skanderbeg's Story* describes the life of Albania's national hero.

In the early 1900s, critic, translator, and politician Faik Konica founded the magazine *Albania*. Albanians throughout Europe read this journal. Bishop Fan Noli wrote histories of Albania after he was forced to leave the country. He also translated the works of

William Shakespeare, Edgar Allen Poe, and Henry Wadsworth Longfellow into Albanian.

Albania's Communist government used drama to promote its policies. Playwrights celebrated the achievements of Socialism and the heroism of Albania's World War II resistance fighters. The country's first professional theater company began in Shkodër in 1949. Since then theater companies have sprung up in several other Albanian cities.

Ismail Kadare

The novels of Ismail Kadare, Albania's best-known modern author, have appeared in more than twenty languages. His books include *The General of the Dead Army* (1963) and *Chronicle in Stone* (1971). Ledia Dushi has published several volumes of poetry in the dialect of Shkodër, where she was born. Flutura Açka, a journalist and poet, has published several poetry collections and one novel in the 1990s and early 2000s. She founded Skanderbeg Books in Tiranë. This company publishes the works of both Albanian and foreign authors.

Religion

Before Communism, about two-thirds of Albanians were Muslim and one-third were Christian. Under Communist rule, few Albanians dared to practice their religion openly. The government closed mosques and churches. It converted some into homes, warehouses, or gyms. In 1967 Enver Hoxha outlawed religion entirely. For two decades, Albania's religious leaders suffered imprisonment, exile, and execution.

Muslim women in Albania greet one another with a customary kiss on the cheek.

This Eastern Orthodox church is in Korçë. The city is home to a large population of Orthodox Christians.

Many Albanians continued to worship in private, however. Religious faith survived. In May 1990, the legislature reversed Hoxha's decree. Soon Muslims and Christians were opening schools, holding services, and attracting new believers.

About 70 percent of Albanians are Muslims. Muslims believe that Allah (God) gave messages to his prophet (spiritual spokesperson) Muhammad through the angel Gabriel in the A.D. 600s. The holy scriptures of the Quran contain these messages. Muslims strive to fulfill the five pillars, or central duties, of Islam: faith in Allah and his prophet Muhammad; praying five times daily; giving charity; fasting during the holy month of Ramadan; and visiting the holy city of Mecca, Saudi Arabia, once in a lifetime, if possible.

About one-fourth of Albanian Muslims have connections to the Bektashi sect, a form of Islamic mysticism. (Mystics follow emotional, intellectual, and physical practices as a path to God.) Hajji Bektash Wali founded the sect in Turkey in the 1200s. When Turkey outlawed Bektashism in the early 1900s, many Bektashi migrated to Albania.

Albania's highlands stayed untouched by many of the events and trends of the lowlands. When Christianity and Islam arrived, Albanian highlanders held to their ancient Illyrian paganism, worshipping various gods of nature. Some pagan beliefs and customs survived to the present. Albania's Spring Day festival is one key example.

The remaining 30 percent of Albanians are mostly Christians. When the Great Schism split Christianity into two main branches in 1054, the boundary between the two ran right through Albania. The Tosks of southern Albania generally adopted Eastern Orthodox

Christianity. About two-thirds of modern Albania's Christians belong to the Eastern Orthodox Church. The Ghegs of northern Albania generally adopted Roman Catholicism. About one-third of modern Albania's Christians are Catholics.

Unlike their neighbors in several other Balkan countries, Christians and Muslims in Albania live together peacefully. Members of one faith often join the religious observances and celebrations of the other.

Food

Traditional Albanian food resembles Greek and Turkish cuisine. Lunch is the day's main meal. At the beginning of a meal, diners may enjoy a plate of *meza* (appetizers) offering cheese, olives, cured meats, and sausages. The main meal may include salad, meat, pasta, rice, and bread. The most popular meats are beef, chicken, sausage, and fish. Many dishes feature green and red peppers, cucumbers, tomatoes, and feta cheese, a crumbly white cheese made from sheep or goat milk. The mild climate of the coast allows Albanian farmers to grow many different vegetables and fruits. These add variety to Albanian cuisine.

The national dish of Albania is *tavë kosi*. It is a baked dish of lamb, yogurt, eggs, and rice. Albanians also enjoy *byrek*, a dish made from wafer-thin leaves of pastry filled with cheese, meat, or vegetables.

In Albania breakfast often includes *kabuni* and *paça*. Kabuni is a sweet pilaf of rice, raisins, sugar, and spices such as cinnamon and cloves. Paça is a garlicky soup made with animals' innards. Baklava

This table at an Albanian farmhouse is full of various traditional foods, including vegetables, cheese, eggs, and meat.

JANI ME FASULE (BEAN STEW)

2 cups of dry white beans
½ cup chopped onion
¼ cup olive oil
2 tablespoons tomato sauce

1 tablespoon chopped parsley
salt to taste
chili powder to taste (about 1 teaspoon
1 tablespoon chopped mint

1. Put beans in a large pot with enough water to completely cover them. Over medium heat, bring the beans to a boil and continue boiling, uncovered, for 5 minutes.
2. Drain and rinse the beans. Put them back in the pot with 3 cups of water. Bring the beans to a boil again and continue boiling for another 15 minutes—this time covered.
3. In a skillet over medium heat, sauté onion in olive oil until it turns yellow. Add 2 tablespoons of liquid from the bean pot, tomato sauce, parsley, salt, and chili powder. Simmer for 10 minutes, or until a thick sauce forms.
4. Pour onion mixture into the bean pot. Add chopped mint. Cover tightly and simmer for 2 hours over low heat. This should produce a thick stew, with just a little liquid covering the beans.
5. Serve hot.

Serves 4

is a favorite dessert. It is made of finely chopped nuts and honey or syrup between layers of paper-thin pastry.

Albanians usually drink strong, dark, sweet coffee after meals. Adults may enjoy white and red wines from the Durrës region or an after-dinner drink called *raki*. Raki is a strong brandy made from fermented grapes or plums.

These men at a café in Gjirokastër are deep in conversation over cups of strong Albanian coffee.

The mountains make a scenic backdrop for these **boys playing soccer** in northeastern Albania.

Sports

Soccer is the favorite sport of Albanians. Like most people outside the United States, Albanians call this sport football. The first club formed in Shkodër. The Albanian Football Association began holding matches among six teams in 1930. Under Communism, towns, schools, and businesses across the country formed football teams. The sport provided easy, inexpensive recreation and entertainment for many poor people.

During the 1990s, several Albanian football stars moved to play for professional teams elsewhere in Europe. Albania's national team competes in the Union of European Football Associations (UEFA). In 2004 Albania scored two surprise victories against Russia and Georgia in the UEFA championship qualifying round.

Albanian schools sponsor not only football but also volleyball, basketball, and wrestling squads. Fans follow matches in all these sports on television and radio. Along the coast, sport diving and swimming are popular. The rugged countryside offers challenging and scenic mountain climbing and hiking.

Albania sent twenty-seven athletes to the 2008 Olympic Games in Beijing, China. They competed in swimming, track, weight lifting, wrestling, judo, and shooting. These games were the fourth Olympic competition for Klodiana Shala, a runner.

Holidays and Festivals

Albania celebrates several public holidays. New Year's Day falls on January 1 and 2. On March 14, Albanians observe the ancient festival of Spring Day, which celebrates the rebirth of nature after a long

Students at the University of Tiranë dance in a **Labor Day celebration.**

winter. Labor Day, a celebration of workers, takes place on May 1. Mother Teresa Day on October 19 honors the Albanian nun famous throughout the world for her charitable work in India. Independence Day falls on November 28. It marks Albania's freedom from Ottoman rule. Liberation Day on November 29 recalls the end of Italian and German occupation of Albania during World War II.

Albanian Muslims celebrate Islasmic holidays. These follow a lunar, or moon, calendar, so their dates change each year. The two most important are Ramadan Bajram and Kurban Bajram. Ramadan Bajram happens at the end of the holy month of Ramadan. During the daylight hours of Ramadan, Muslims fast (avoid eating and drinking) to honor Allah's revelation of the Quran to Muhammad. On Ramadan Bajram, Muslims celebrate with feasting, praying, and family gatherings. Kurban Bajram honors the biblical Abraham's willingness to sacrifice his son to Allah.

For Albanian Christians, Easter is the most important religious holiday. It takes place on varying dates in the spring. During the week before Easter, families attend a series of church services. Albanians celebrate Easter Sunday with a feast that includes brightly colored eggs and sweet bread shaped into a circle or two braids. Christmas (December 25) is another important holiday for Albanian Christians. Families celebrate with gift giving, Christmas trees, and church services. The Christmas feast always includes baklava.

Visit www.vgsbooks.com for links to websites with more information about Albania's culture.

THE ECONOMY

Before World War II, Albania had a farming economy. Albanians depended on neighboring nations for manufactured goods. It had only a handful of small factories. The road system was poor, and most of the country lacked electricity.

Communism transformed Albania's economy. The government took control of farms and businesses. It began a central economic planning system. A series of five-year plans set high production goals for factories and collective farms. The government began investing in roads, bridges, ports, and other infrastructure.

The government wanted to create a completely self-sufficient nation. But as Albania grew more isolated, its foreign trade ended. Albania grew poorer. Wages fell, along with government investment in industry and energy. Albania broke its alliances with the Soviet Union and China. As a result, the country lost much-needed foreign aid.

In the early 1990s, a new government began to privatize the economy. The state sold off farmland to private farmers and factories to

foreign firms. Private companies, many of them Italian, made loans to help new Albanian businesses.

In the twenty-first century, Albania's gross domestic product (GDP), the total value of goods and services produced each year inside Albania, is $6,200 per person. The economy is growing 6 percent per year. This rate is faster than the European average. But Albania still struggles with high unemployment. At least 12 percent of Albanians can't find work. Many workers move abroad for better opportunities.

In 2008 an economic crisis struck the United States and then spread to Europe and the rest of the world. The crisis caused an international recession—a drop in employment, profits, production, and sales. Lending to Albania by foreign banks and companies nearly disappeared.

Albania also runs a trade deficit, meaning Albanians and their government buy more goods from foreign countries than they sell. This makes it difficult for them to spend money on new businesses and infrastructure.

TOURIST ATTRACTIONS

Albania has many tourist attractions. The Ionian coast offers quiet beaches. Durrës boasts the region's largest Roman amphitheater. Butrint *(below)* and Apollonia also have important archaeological sites. Well-preserved Ottoman buildings line the steep, winding streets of Berat and Gjirokastër. Adventurous tourists can visit the rugged mountains and trek through the highlands to the eastern lakes.

⊙ Services

Services are all business activities that provide useful labor instead of material goods. This sector includes banking, insurance, shipping and transportation, hotels and restaurants, tourism, business services, wholesale and retail trade, telecommunications, construction, and government services. The service sector employs about 27 percent of the working population and makes up 60 percent of GDP.

Albania's service sector expanded after the fall of Communism. This sector has attracted investment from foreign countries, such as Italy and Greece. The banking and insurance sectors are growing. In addition, Albania's low wages attract foreign firms that want to outsource (pay others to do) their office tasks, such as data entry and customer service. Hotels, restaurants, and shops meet a growing demand for goods and services in the cities.

The government of Albania began allowing tourists to visit during the 1980s. Tourism grew after Communism fell. Italian, German, and Middle Eastern companies built new hotels and resorts in Albania. Tourism continues to grow almost 4 percent per year.

⊙ Agriculture

After Communist rule ended, Albania's new government set up village councils. These councils returned all collective land to private farmers by 1993. Agriculture contributes about 21 percent to modern Albania's GDP and employs 58 percent of the workforce. Albania's agricultural sector includes farming, fishing, and forestry.

A farmer plows his field in the Vjosë River valley. Agriculture has long played a vital role in Albania's economy.

About 70 percent of Albania is mountainous. Most of the land is unsuitable for farming. Most farmland lies in the coastal lowlands. The flat terrain and the mild climate there help farmers grow cotton, sugar beets, tomatoes, grapes, citrus fruits, rice, wheat, potatoes, and corn.

Farming also occurs in the small basins and fertile valleys scattered throughout Albania. In the Korçë Basin, for example, olive trees thrive. Farmers raise livestock—including sheep, poultry, goats, cattle, hogs, and horses—in highland pastures and in the valleys and basins among the mountains.

Albania's forests supply wood to the nation's construction companies. In addition, many households burn wood for cooking and heat. Overcutting has caused deforestation, erosion, and loss of wildlife habitat. In many once-wooded areas, only shoots and shrubs survive. A small reforestation project is under way, but Albania continues to cut trees faster than it replaces them.

Durrës, Sarandë, Vlorë, and Shëngjin are Albania's main fishing ports. The government is building new seawalls, docks, fueling stations, and public markets to boost the fishing industry. New hatcheries

URBAN FARMING

Many urban Albanian families tend small gardens in their backyards or on their roofs. They use large pots, bowls, or paint cans to grow tomatoes, peppers, onions, cucumbers, and cabbage. They pickle vegetables in brine to preserve them and hang onions and garlic to dry. Some city dwellers also keep livestock such as chickens, goats, or sheep. A small flock of family sheep grazing beside a busy road is a common sight in Albanian towns.

and dock facilities operate on the inland lakes too. Albanian fish farms raise freshwater and saltwater species—including mussels, shrimp, trout, carp, and bass—for public markets and for export.

Industry

In modern Albania, industry (including manufacturing, mining, and energy) contributes 19 percent of the nation's GDP and employs 15 percent of the labor force. The government has closed many inefficient factories. Those still operating make building materials, furniture, textiles, shoes, cigarettes, televisions, and radios. Food processors prepare bread, wine, beer, olive oil, and sugar. Industrial plants produce chemicals and refined metals. Oil refineries make gasoline, kerosene, fuel oil, and asphalt.

Minerals earn substantial export income for Albania. The nation has several chromite mines. Chromite, refined into chromium, is a key ingredient in stainless steel. Automobiles, appliances, and heavy machinery all require chromium. Rising chromite production and chromium refining have made Albania a top international supplier of this metal. Albania also mines copper and phosphate (used in fertilizer, baking powder, and toothpaste).

Albania has deposits of natural gas, petroleum, and coal. It extracts and refines some coal and oil but has not yet exploited its natural gas. Albania is working with Italy and Saudi Arabia to explore offshore oil reserves. In 2008 engineers discovered a large oil deposit in northern

These women work in a textile factory in Shkodër.

Albania. This discovery might allow Albania to begin exporting crude oil.

More than 80 percent of Albania's electricity comes from its hydroelectric plants on the Drin and Mat rivers. Fossil fuels such as coal and oil generate the rest. Albanian power plants produce enough electricity for export. But the country's transmission system is inefficient. Power outages are frequent. Some small towns and villages do not have access to electricity.

Foreign Trade

Greece, Germany, Turkey, and Italy are Albania's chief trading partners. Albania imports machinery, fuels, chemicals, food, and consumer goods from these nations. Italian companies also provide cars and technicians. Greece sells food products particularly in Tiranë and southern Albania. Albania buys more goods and services from abroad than it sells to foreign countries.

Italy is the major market for Albanian exports. Albania also sells chromite, electricity, copper wire, tobacco, and oil to the Czech Republic, Bulgaria, and Germany.

Thousands of Albanians who work abroad send money back to their relatives in Albania. These remittances make up a large portion of Albania's export income. The low cost of labor in Albania has attracted several foreign companies to set up branches there.

Albania no longer isolates itself from the world economy. As a result, the country shares in global economic problems. The worldwide slump that began in 2008 has cut Albanian exports.

Transportation

Albania's road network consists of about 11,185 miles (18,000 km) of two-lane paved and unpaved roads. A few freeways link the main ports

FURGON IT

A common way to get from place to place in Albania is to use a *furgon*. This is a van or minibus that waits at busy intersections in the cities. A small sign in the window tells its destination. The van sells no tickets. The driver just waits until all the seats are filled and then starts driving toward the destination. The passengers yell out their stops along the way. When passengers get off, the driver charges them for the time they've been aboard.

with Tiranë. About 40 percent of the roads are paved. Roads are poor in the highlands. Motor vehicles cannot reach much of the country.

Albania has five airports—four with paved runways. Tiranë International Airport links Albania with several European nations. The state-owned railway system covers 278 miles (447 km). An international line runs between Shkodër and Podgorica, Montenegro.

Albania's only river that big commercial boats can navigate, the Bojana, links Lake Shkodër with the Adriatic Sea. Passenger ferries link the seaports of Durrës and Vlorë. A small merchant fleet connects Albania's coastal cities with Italian ports.

● Communications

Modern Albania licenses national and local television stations. Albanians pay a small fee each year to receive Radio Televizioni Shqiptar (Albanian Radio and Television), a national public network. It broadcasts radio and TV programming to Albania and Albanian communities in neighboring nations. Foreign broadcasts, including Italy's Radiotelevisione Italiana and the U.S. Cable News Network (CNN), arrive via satellite.

Albania's major newspapers are *Gazeta Shqiptare*, *Korrieri*, and *Shekulli*. These papers follow the lead of the country's major political parties. Albanians look on them as sources of political opinion, not news. For more reliable information, many people turn instead to Internet news services or to radio networks that arrive from outside the country, such as the British Broadcasting Company (BBC).

Radio Tiranë, founded in the 1930s, is still Albania's most popular radio station. It presents music, news, drama, and educational programs. It maintains three stations in Tiranë and local stations in Gjirokastër, Shkodër, and Korçë.

About three million cell phones are in use in Albania—almost one for every citizen. Landline telephone service in Albania is poor. City dwellers must use party lines (shared lines) or go without service. Many villages have no landlines or share a single public telephone. Albania has only about three hundred thousand landline telephones in use.

Albanians gained access to the Internet in the early 2000s. At first Albania had only a few thousand regular users, all of them in Tiranë. In 2007 new Internet service providers started operating, and the number of users reached almost five hundred thousand, or 15 percent of the population. Internet cafés provide the easiest way to get online, for a small fee. Private home connections are expensive and slow.

◯ The Future

Compared to several other Balkan nations, Albania made a fairly smooth and peaceful transition from Communism to democracy. Despite serious economic problems, Albania's new government has stayed stable. Most Albanians support its economic reforms.

Albania struggles with unemployment, and it remains one of the poorest countries in Europe. Corruption scandals, in which government ministers admitted accepting bribes, have plagued Albania's government. Organized criminal gangs operate in many Albanian cities and have expanded to other European countries. Albania is struggling to grow its economy without damaging its environment.

A peaceful transition to democratic government and steady—if slow—economic growth since the early 1990s may not have brought great material benefits, but they have prepared Albania for the struggles ahead. With wise use of its valuable resources, Albania has high hopes for a bright future.

 Visit www.vgsbooks.com for links to websites with more information about Albania's economy.

2000 B.C.	Greek-speaking settlers migrate south through the western Balkan Peninsula.
1000 B.C.	Illyrian society takes shape on the Balkan Peninsula.
600s B.C.	Greek colonists begin building Apollonia and Epidamnos.
300s B.C.	Illyrian kings Bardyllis and Glaucias battle the Greeks.
168 B.C.	Illyria becomes the Roman province of Illyricum.
A.D. 100s	The Roman Empire peaks. Christianity spreads through the empire.
395	The Roman Empire splits into eastern and western halves. Illyria, in turn, divides into northern and southern regions.
500s	Illyrians begin calling themselves Albanians. Slavs invade the Balkan Peninsula.
800s	Albania becomes part of the Bulgarian Empire.
1014	Albania becomes part of the Byzantine Empire.
1054	Albanian Christians split into northern (Roman Catholic) and southern (Eastern Orthodox) branches.
LATE 1000s–EARLY 1300s	Coastal and central Albania suffer a series of invasions and occupations by Italian and Serbian realms.
1300s	The Albanian Balsic, Kastrioti, and Dukagjini clans establish powerful domains.
1400s	The Ottoman Empire conquers Albania.
1443	Skanderbeg, an Albanian officer in the Ottoman army, turns against the Turks, sparking a twenty-year resistance against Turkish rule.
1468	Skanderbeg dies, and Albania soon falls again to the Ottoman Turks.
1500s–1600s	Albanian Christians suffer persecution. Many Albanians seek better lives by becoming Muslims and working for the Ottoman government.
LATE 1700s	The Ottoman Empire begins to weaken.
1878	After a war between Russia and Turkey, treaties establish new independent Balkan nations. Albania stays in the Ottoman Empire. Albanians form the League of Prizren to seek self-rule.
1881	The Ottoman army defeats the League of Prizren.
1909–1911	Albanian independence fighters force out Turkish troops.
1912	Albanian leaders declare the country's independence.
1913	European powers recognize Albanian independence and appoint German prince Wilhelm zu Wied as king of Albania. Albanians accept this plan.

1914   Essad Pasha forms a rebel army to oppose Prince Wilhelm.

1914-1918   World War I takes place. Several nations battle for control of Balkan territory. After the war, the Allies meet in Paris and agree to divide Albania among Greece, Italy, and the new nation of Yugoslavia.

1920   Albanian leaders meet at Lushnjë, reject the Paris agreement, and again declare Albania's independence. The United States supports Albania.

1920-1924   Liberals under Fan Noli and conservatives under Ahmed Zogu wrestle for control of the government. Zogu eventually succeeds.

1925-1938   Zogu declares himself president, then all-powerful king. Albania allies with Italy, inspiring an Albanian Communist opposition movement.

1939-1945   World War II takes place. Italian and German troops invade and occupy Albania. After the war, Albania becomes a Communist state under Enver Hoxha.

1955   Albania joins the Warsaw Pact, a Soviet-led Communist alliance.

1961   Albania cuts off relations with the Soviet Union and allies itself with China.

1970s   Albania cracks down on opposition; outlaws religion; bans foreign media, travel, and trade; and cuts ties with China.

1985   Hoxha dies. Ramiz Alia succeeds him. Albania gradually loosens its strict policies.

1990   Rioting and mass emigration force the government to draw up a new constitution and to allow multiparty elections.

1992-1997   The Democratic Party in Albania wins control of the legislature and the presidency. The government lifts travel and trade restrictions and privatizes the economy.

1997   A government-approved investment scheme crumbles, taking many Albanians' life savings with it. Rioting ensues, thousands die, and the government nearly collapses. This disaster shifts government control to the Socialist Party.

1999   Ongoing conflict in the Serbian province of Kosovo erupts into war. Albania supports Kosovo's fight for independence from Serbia.

2002   Alfred Moisiu, a politically neutral president, takes power in Albania.

2007   Albania's Democratic Party regains control of the government.

2008   Albania is the first nation to recognize Kosovo's independence.

2009   Albania becomes a NATO member and applies for EU membership. The Democratic Party wins legislative elections by a slim margin.

2010   EU officials urge Albania to resolve its legislative problems, which could jeopardize its entry into the EU.

COUNTRY NAME Republic of Albania

AREA 11,100 square miles (28,748 sq. km)

MAIN LANDFORMS Central Highlands, Coastal Lowlands, Cukali Highlands, Eastern Highlands, Korçë Basin, Myzeque Plain, North Albanian Alps, Southern Highlands

HIGHEST POINT Mount Korab, 9,068 feet (2,764 m) above sea level

LOWEST POINT sea level

MAJOR RIVERS Bojana, Drin, Drino, Mat, Shkumbin, Vjosë

ANIMALS brown bears, capercaillies, chamois, cormorants, deer, ducks, foxes, golden eagles, gray wolves, hares, herons, lynx, monk seal, otters, partridges, pelicans, pheasants, sea turtles, sturgeon, swans, vultures, wild boars, wild goats

CAPITAL CITY Tiranë

OTHER MAJOR CITIES Durrës, Gjirokastër, Shkodër, Vlorë

OFFICIAL LANGUAGE Albanian

MONETARY UNIT lek

Fast Facts

Currency

ALBANIAN CURRENCY

Albania's currency is the lek (plural lekë). Its name honors Lekë Dukagjini, an Albanian prince of the 1400s. Its international currency code is ALL, and its written symbol is L. The nation mints coins of 1, 5, 10, 20, 50, and 100 lekë. Banknotes come in denominations of 100, 200, 500, 1,000, 2,000, and 5,000 lekë. The 5,000-lekë note has a portrait of the national hero, Skanderbeg, on one side and his fortress, Cërujë Castle, on the other.

The Albanian flag shows a black double-headed eagle on a red background. This symbol originated with Skanderbeg's rebellion for independence from the Ottomans in the 1400s. Albania's leaders adopted the flag on November 28, 1912, upon declaring independence. The flag's details changed several times as regimes rose and fell, but each design preserved the black double-headed eagle and the red field. It remains the world's only national red and black flag.

Albania adopted its national anthem, "Rreth Flamurit të Përbashkuar," or "United around Our Flag," in 1912. The Albanian poet Aleksander Stavre Drenova wrote the words. Romanian composer Ciprian Porumbescu wrote the music. Here are the first two verses of the anthem.

Rreth Flamurit të Përbashkuar
Rreth flamurit të përbashkuar,
Me një dëshirë dhe një qëllim,
Të gjithë Atij duke iu betuar,
Të lidhim besën për shpëtim.

Prej lufte veç ay largohet,
Që është lindur tradhëtor,
Kush është burrë nuk friksohet,
Po vdes, po vdes si një dëshmor.

United around Our Flag
United around the flag,
With one desire and one goal,
Let us pledge our word of honor
To fight for our salvation.

Only he who is a born traitor
Turns from the struggle.
He who is brave is not daunted,
But falls—a martyr to the cause.

 For a link to a site where you can listen to Albania's national anthem, visit www.vgsbooks.com.

SALI BERISHA (b. 1944) Berisha is a prominent Albanian politician. Born in the village of Viçidol, he later became a cardiologist, or heart doctor, and a professor at the University of Tiranë. He became the leader of the Democratic Party in 1991. He served as president of Albania from 1992 to 1997. He became the nation's prime minister in 2005.

ENVER HOXHA (1908–1985) Hoxha was Albania's Communist leader for forty years. Born in Gjirokastër, Hoxha adopted Communist ideals of social equality during the 1930s. He was a resistance fighter during World War II. He emerged as the leader of the Albanian Communist Party during the war and became prime minister in 1944. Over the years, despite his lofty ideals, he isolated Albania from the world, put in place disastrous economic policies, and cracked down harshly on all opponents.

ISMAIL KADARE (b. 1936) Kadare is a renowned Albanian novelist. Born in Gjirokastër, Kadare began his writing career while Albania was an isolated Communist nation. In subtle ways, he never stopped criticizing the government in his novels. He faced many death threats from the government and finally fled Albania for France in 1990. His best-known book, *The General of the Dead Army*, describes the many tragedies of World War II in Albania. Kadare has written nearly twenty novels and has won several important literary awards.

MARIE LOGORECI (1920–1988) Logoreci was a beloved Albanian actress and singer. Born in Shkodër, when she was a young woman, she became a folksinger. She appeared on radio programs in the 1940s and began her acting career on the stage of the National Theater of Albania. The award-winning short movie *Skanderbeg* (1953) gave her her first film role.

FAN NOLI (1882–1965) Noli was an important Albanian religious and political leader. He was born in the Turkish village of Ibrik Tepe. He lived for several years in Boston, Massachusetts, where he became a priest, a leader of the Albanian-American community, and a Harvard University graduate. He established the Albanian Orthodox Church in 1922, became a bishop in 1923, and became prime minister of Albania in 1924. Opponents overthrew his government a few months later, and Noli fled the country. He remained a church leader and a spokesperson for Albanian causes in Europe and the United States.

EDI RAMA (b. 1964) Rama became mayor of Tiranë in 2000. He is also the leader of the Socialist Party. He was born in Tiranë and trained as an artist. He has given exhibitions of his work throughout Europe. He was a professor at Tiranë's Academy of Arts and led the student movement against the Communist regime in the early 1990s. In 2004 he won the World Mayor Award, bestowed by the City Mayors organization for outstanding service as a city leader. He has led a concerted effort to clean up and beautify the capital.

HAVA REXHA (1880–2003) Rexha achieved fame for living an extremely long life. Some people believe she was the longest-lived human ever. She claimed to have been born in 1880 in the village of Shushicë. Her birth date appeared on an official government document issued in 1946. But experts required better proof of her true age, so her longevity is not officially recognized.

KLODIANA SHALA (b. 1979) Shala is a world-class Albanian runner. She was born in Tiranë. She competes in the 200-meter and 400-meter sprints. Shala has competed in four Olympic Games. At the 2004 games in Athens, Greece, she served as the Albanian team's flag bearer.

SKANDERBEG (1405–1468) Skanderbeg is Albania's national hero. He was born in Dibër county in northeastern Albania. His original name was Gjergj Kastrioti. Taken hostage as a boy by Turkish conquerors, he eventually became a general in the Ottoman army. In 1443 he rallied a force of Albanian fighters to liberate Albania from the Ottoman Empire. This force turned back more than a dozen Turkish invasions before Skanderbeg died of malaria. Albania commemorates his heroism with statues and memorials in all its major towns.

MOTHER TERESA (1910–1997) Mother Teresa was an Albanian nun famous for her charitable work in India. She was born Agnesë Gonxhe Bojaxhiu in Skopje, Macedonia, to an Albanian family from Shkodër. She became a Catholic nun at the age of eighteen. From 1950 until a few months before her death, she led the Missionaries of Charity in Calcutta, India, which she founded. She established new branches of the mission throughout the world, helping orphans, lepers, the poor, and people with HIV/AIDS. She won the Nobel Peace Prize in 1979.

APOLLONIA Archaeologists are conducting an ongoing dig at this ancient Greek city in southwestern Albania. Its ruins include a house of mosaics (pictures made from tiny colored pieces of tile), a bouleuterion (city council chamber), a library, a triumphal arch, a temple, and an odeum (theater).

BERAT Berat is a well-preserved historic town on the Osum River in south central Albania. The many old homes rising from the riverbank give it the nickname city of a thousand windows. The ruined Berat Castle, from Illyrian times, stands on a rugged hill just outside the town.

BUTRINT Albania founded Butrint National Park in southern Albania to protect the Greek, Byzantine, and Ottoman ruins of this site. Butrint also includes breathtaking scenery and a rare and complex ecosystem (community of living things).

CËRUJË This city is the site of a historic hilltop fortress built during the 1400s. Skanderbeg made it his headquarters during his campaign against the Ottoman Turks. Inside the restored castle, the Skanderbeg Museum displays relics from the hero's life and times. Cërujë is also home to a restored Ottoman bazaar (market).

DURRËS This port city is growing fast as a seaside resort for Albanians and tourists. Visitors can walk on a seaside promenade and visit the Balkan region's largest ancient Roman amphitheater. Durrës also holds the palace of King Zog.

GJIROKASTËR This well-preserved historic town lies on the Drino River in southern Albania. It is not only scenic but is also home to many Byzantine and Ottoman buildings. Gjirokastër Castle, a hilltop fortress built in the 1700s, overlooks the town. A military museum and a former prison are inside the fort. On its walls sits a U.S. Air Force spy plane captured in the 1960s.

KORÇË This city in southeastern Albania holds many historic buildings, including a *han* (inn) once used by Ottoman traders from central Asia. The inn remains in business as a hotel. Korçë is also home to several museums, as well as beautiful old churches and mosques.

TIRANË The bustling capital of Albania has several grand avenues displaying statues, murals, and architecture from the Communist period. The Blloku neighborhood is a shopping and nightlife hot spot. Skanderbeg Square, the heart of the city, holds a towering statue of Skanderbeg. The city also offers numerous museums, theaters, churches, mosques, and other cultural attractions.

VLORË This city overlooks a wide bay on the Strait of Otranto. Swimming beaches attract vacationers, who can also enjoy walks in the oak forests on the surrounding hillsides.

bora: a cold, strong wind that blows across Albania from the north or the northeast

chromite: a metal ore refined to produce chromium, a key ingredient in stainless steel. Chromite mining and processing are mainstays of Albania's economy.

clan: in Albania a group of families allied for self-defense and to enforce a social code

Communism: a political and economic theory that envisions community ownership of all property. Its goal is to create equality, but in practice, Communist rule has strictly limited personal freedoms and economic growth. Albania had a Communist government from 1945 to 1992.

conservatives: people who support established institutions and cultural norms and who generally favor a limited role for government. In political spheres, conservatives are often called the Right. In newly independent Albania, conservatives favored landowner control of the government and the economy.

constitution: a document defining the basic principles and laws of a nation

deforestation: loss of woodlands due to logging or clearing land for farming, construction, or other human uses. Deforestation leads to soil erosion, loss of wildlife habitat, and global warming.

democracy: government by the people, through free elections

feudal: a system in which landowners claimed the farm production and military service of people who lived on their land

hydroelectricity: electricity produced by damming a river and then harnessing the energy of rushing water at power stations. Hydroelectric dams provide most of Albania's electricity.

land reclamation: the process of creating farmland from riverbeds, seabeds, or wetlands

liberals: people who support the idea that institutions and cultural norms can change as societal attitudes shift and who generally support a broad role for government. In political spheres, liberals are often called the Left.

lignite: a soft brown variety of coal. Albania burns lignite in some of its electrical power plants. Its smoke causes air pollution.

paganism: the ancient, pre-Christian religion of the Illyrians, who worshipped different gods of nature

recession: a period of reduced economic activity marked by a drop in employment, profits, production, and sales

Socialism: an economic and political system in which groups of workers or the nation as a whole—not individuals—own the nation's resources and its means of production. Socialism is one stage on the way to full Communism.

Selected Bibliography

AlbanianEconomy.com. **N.d.**
http://www.albanianeconomy.com/news (March 23, 2010).
This online news agency provides constantly updated information on economic affairs in Albania and the Balkan region.

Carver, Robert. *The Accursed Mountains: Journeys in Albania.* **New York: HarperCollins, 1998.**
The author of this book, a British journalist, recalls his travels through the rural Albanian highlands in 1996. He describes not only the wild beauty of the land and the independence of its people but also poverty, chaos, and the constant threat of violence.

Durham, M. Edith. *High Albania.* **Gloucester, UK: Dodo Press, 2008.**
A British anthropologist wrote this memoir of her time in Albania in 1909, when Albania was still under Ottoman control and fighting for independence. The author describes Albanian social customs, religious practices, and history.

Jacques, Edwin E. *The Albanians: An Ethnic History from Prehistoric Times to the Present.* **Jefferson, NC: McFarland, 2009.**
This book describes the struggle of Albanians to preserve their culture through centuries of war and occupation.

Pearson, Owen. *Albania in the Twentieth Century: A History.* **London: Center for Albanian Studies, 2004–2006.**
This three-volume history offers a detailed and scholarly account of 1900s Albania. It begins with the drive for independence and ends with the Kosovo War.

Population Reference Bureau. **March 18, 2010.**
http://www.prb.org (March 23, 2010).
The bureau offers current population figures, vital statistics, land area, and more. Special articles cover the latest environmental and health issues that concern each country, including Albania.

Tomes, Jason. *King Zog of Albania: Europe's Self-Made Muslim Monarch.* **New York: New York University Press, 2004.**
This biography of Albania's King Zog describes how Ahmed Zogu fashioned his own kingdom and ruled it with cunning and cruelty during a chaotic period of Albanian history.

Vickers, Miranda. *Between Serb and Albanian: A History of Kosovo.* **New York: Columbia University Press, 1998.**
The author describes the centuries-old ethnic conflicts between Muslim Albanians and Christian Serbs in Kosovo, Albania's northeastern neighbor.

Vickers, Miranda, and James Pettifer. *Albania: From Anarchy to a Balkan Identity.* **New York: New York University Press, 1997.**
This book describes the drastic changes that occurred in Albania just before and during the fall of its Communist regime.

The World Factbook. **March 4, 2010.**
https://www.cia.gov/library/publications/the-world-factbook/geos/al.html (March 23, 2010).
This website of the U.S. Central Intelligence Agency features up-to-date information about the people, the land, the economy, and the government of Albania. It also briefly covers transnational issues.

Zickel, Raymond E., and Walter Iwaskiw. *Albania: A Country Study.* **Washington, DC: U.S. Government Printing Office, 1994.**
This is a comprehensive handbook on Albania's geography, climate, history, economy, society, political affairs, and culture.

Albania Internet Information Center
http://www.findalbanian.com
This portal offers links to dozens of websites on Albanian news, entertainment, sports, and events.

Albanian Daily News
http://www.albaniannews.com
This online newspaper presents in English the latest events and information from Albania.

Country Profile: Albania
http://news.bbc.co.uk/2/hi/europe/country_profiles/1004234.stm
This helpful site provides a quick overview of Albania's recent history, political events, and economic development. It also provides links to related topics.

Durham, M. Edith. *Albania and the Albanians: Selected Articles and Letters 1903–1944.* **London: I. B. Tauris, 2005.**
This book is a collection of essays by a respected twentieth-century traveler and historian of the Balkan region. Durham witnessed and studied many important events in the early 1900s in Albania.

Elsie, Robert. *Balkan Beauty, Balkan Blood: Modern Albanian Short Stories.* **Evanston, IL: Northwestern University Press, 2006.**
This anthology offers stories from several major Albanian authors working since the 1980s.

Elsie, Robert, and Janice Mathie-Heck. *Lightning from the Depths: An Anthology of Albanian Poetry.* **Evanston, IL: Northwestern University Press, 2008.**
This collection offers hundreds of poems by major Albanian writers spanning six centuries.

Goldstein, Margaret J. *World War II: Europe.* **Minneapolis: Twenty-First Century Books, 2004.**
This book gives a detailed overview of the events of World War II in Europe.

Hodgkinson, Harry. *Scanderbeg: From Ottoman Captive to Albanian Hero.* **London: I. B. Tauris, 2005.**
The author presents a complete biography of Albania's national hero, from his youth as an Ottoman captive to his revolts against Ottoman rule in the 1400s.

Jones, Lloyd. *Biografi: A Traveler's Tale.* **Orlando, FL: Harcourt Brace, 1993.**
In this novel written as a travelogue, a journalist visits Albania just as the Communist government falls and Albanians struggle to overcome their isolation and create a new nation.

Kadare, Ismail. *The General of the Dead Army.* **New York: Vintage Classics, 2009.**
This famous novel tells the story of an Italian officer searching through Albania for the bodies of soldiers killed during World War II.

Knowlton, Mary Lee. *Albania.* Tarrytown, NY: Marshall Cavendish Benchmark, 2005.

This book for younger readers includes basic information on Albanian history, geography, culture, and economic life.

Loring, Ian, and Paul Alkazraji. *Christ and the Kalashnikov: Stories of Hope in War-Torn Albania.* London: Marshall Pickering, 2001.

This book describes the struggle of foreign Christian missionaries (religious teachers) to cope with the chaos and violence that broke out in Albania in 1997, after a financial scandal affected the entire population.

Mangerich, Agnes Jensen. *Albanian Escape: The True Story of U.S. Army Nurses Behind Enemy Lines.* Lexington: University Press of Kentucky, 2006.

A plane carrying a group of World War II U.S. Army nurses goes down over Albania behind German lines. With the help of Albanian underground fighters, the group treks over 800 miles (1,287 km) to reach safety.

Oakley-Hill, D. R. *An Englishman in Albania: Memoirs of a British Officer, 1929–1955.* London: I. B. Tauris, 2005.

A British officer describes his experiences in Albania in the mid-1900s, including encounters with Albanian leaders King Zog and Enver Hoxha.

Pettifer, James. *Albania and Kosovo: Blue Guide.* London: A & C Black, 2001.

This guide to historic sites and monuments in Albania offers the reader a series of road trips with detailed information on the local history back to ancient times.

Sherman, Josepha. *The Cold War.* Minneapolis: Twenty-First Century Books, 2004.

This entry in the Chronicle of America's Wars series discusses the events leading up to and defining the Cold War.

Tarifa, Fatos. *To Albania, with Love.* Lanham, MD: Hamilton Books, 2007.

This memoir chronicles the career of the author, a prominent Albanian sociologist, university professor, and former ambassador to the United States.

vgsbooks.com
http://www.vgsbooks.com

Visit vgsbooks.com, the home page of the Visual Geography Series®. You can get linked to all sorts of useful online information, including geographical, historical, demographic, cultural, and economic websites. The vgsbooks.com site is a great resource for late-breaking news and statistics about many nations, including Albania.

Welcome to Albania
http://www.albaniantourism.com

This online guide provides tourists information on Albania's interesting cities and historical sites. It also offers a currency converter, weather reports, a traveler's forum, and up-to-date information on the country's cultural scene.

Captions for photos appearing on cover and chapter openers:

Cover: Hillside houses overlook a valley in the historic town of Gjirokastër.

pp. 4–5 Albania's southern coast borders the Ionian Sea. Sandy beaches line the shore.

pp. 8–9 The North Albanian Alps stretch from northern Albania into eastern Montenegro.

pp. 38–39 These friends from Gjirokastër are all smiles.

pp. 46–47 Four women in northwestern Albania, dressed in traditional Albanian clothing, stop for a photo.

pp. 58–59 Tourists take advantage of a sunny day along the Adriatic Sea by relaxing on this beautiful beach in Durrës.

Photo Acknowledgments
The images in this book are used with the permission of: © Jack Malipan Travel Photography/Alamy, pp. 4–5; © XNR Productions, pp. 6, 10; © Salajean/Dreamstime.com, pp. 8–9; © De Agostini/SuperStock, p. 11; © Erol Houssein/Impact/HIP/The Image Works, p. 12; © bildagentur-online. com/th-foto/Alamy, p. 13; © Silvio Fiore/SuperStock, p. 14; © Peter Treanor/ Art Directors & TRIP, pp. 16, 17, 44, 57; © Brian Gibbs/Art Directors & TRIP, p. 18; © age fotostock/SuperStock, pp. 19, 52 (bottom); © North Wind Picture Archives, pp. 22, 23; © The Print Collector/Heritage/The Image Works, p. 24; © Interfoto/Alamy, p. 26; © RIA Novosti/Alamy, p. 27; © Hulton Deutsch Collection/CORBIS, p. 29; AP Photo, p. 30; AP Photo/Gazetta Shqip, p. 31; © Bettmann/CORBIS, p. 33; AP Photo/at/ L. Lika-ATA, p. 35; © Andrew Testa/Panos Pictures, p. 36 (top); AP Photo/ Cedric Joubert, p. 36 (bottom); © Wolfgang Kaehler, www.wkaehlerphoto. com, pp. 38–39; © Cory Langley, pp. 40, 42; © Tim Dirven/Panos Pictures, p. 41; © Philip Wolmuth/Alamy, p. 43; © Arben Celi/Reuters/CORBIS, p. 45; © Bildagentur/Tips Italia/Photolibrary, pp. 46–47; © Alfredo Caliz/Panos Pictures, p. 48; © Michel Setboun/CORBIS, p. 49; © Robin Graham/Art Directors & TRIP, p. 50; AP Photo/Visar Kryeziu, p. 52 (top); © Travel Ink/ Gallo Images/Getty Images, p. 53; © Crispin Hughes/Panos Pictures, p. 54; © Riccardo Mancioli/Alamy, p. 55; © Alan Gignoux/Alamy, p. 56; © Th-foto Werbung/Art Directors & TRIP, p. 58; © Robert Harding Picture Library/ SuperStock, pp. 60, 61; © Andrea Matone/Alamy, p. 62; © Nick Haslam/ Alamy, p. 63; Images courtesy of Banknotes.com - Audrius Tomonis, p. 68 (all); © Laura Westlund/Independent Picture Service, p. 69.

Front cover: © Chris Sattlberger/Panos Pictures.